The Delivering Power of Love holds a wealth of information, giving Biblical insight to the reasons why an individual may carry years of hurts and pains in their emotions, and, moreover, even sickness and disease around in their bodies. The author takes the reader on a journey to discover the keys to bring about their own personal deliverance, or the the deliverance of another, as well as how to walk daily in freedom from such bondages as torment, fear, trauma, bitterness and unforgivness. Donna Cameron shares her wealth of knowledge gained from years of deliverance ministry and reveals the great love of the Lord Jesus Christ for all people. This book is a must read.

Carol Elaine, Th. D.
Dr. Carol Elaine Ministries

Delivering Power

THE MASTER KEY TO YOUR FREEDOM

Dr. Donna Cameron-Cepeda

TRILOGY CHRISTIAN PUBLISHERS
TUSTIN, CA

Trilogy Christian Publishers
A Wholly Owned Subsidiary of Trinity Broadcasting Network
2442 Michelle Drive
Tustin, CA 92780

Copyright © 2020 by Dr. Donna Cameron-Cepeda

All Scripture quotations, unless otherwise noted, taken from THE HOLY BIBLE, NEW INTERNATIONAL VERSION®, NIV® Copyright © 1973, 1978, 1984, 2011 by Biblica, Inc.® Used by permission. All rights reserved worldwide.

Scripture quotations marked (KJV) taken from The Holy Bible, King James Version. Cambridge Edition: 1769.

All rights reserved, including the right to reproduce this book or portions thereof in any form whatsoever.

For information, address Trilogy Christian Publishing

Rights Department, 2442 Michelle Drive, Tustin, Ca 92780.

Trilogy Christian Publishing/ TBN and colophon are trademarks of Trinity Broadcasting Network.

For information about special discounts for bulk purchases, please contact Trilogy Christian Publishing.

Manufactured in the United States of America

Trilogy Disclaimer: The views and content expressed in this book are those of the author and may not necessarily reflect the views and doctrine of Trilogy Christian Publishing or the Trinity Broadcasting Network.

10 9 8 7 6 5 4 3 2 1

Library of Congress Cataloging-in-Publication Data is available.

ISBN 9978-1-64773-843-3

ISBN 978-1-64773-844-0 (ebook)

Contents

Introduction vii

Chapter One. The Invisible Kingdom 1

Chapter Two. Can a Christian Have an Open Door to the Demonic? 11

Chapter Three. Open Doors to the Demonic 23

Chapter Four. The Strong Man 30

Chapter Five. Bitterness is a Principality 39

Chapter Six. Unholy Thoughts 52

Chapter Seven. Fear vs. Perfect Love 77

Chapter Eight. Demonic Intimidation 92

Chapter Nine. Jesus the Deliverer 106

Chapter Ten. Keep Your Eyes on Jesus 117

Chapter Eleven. Love and Healing 125

Chapter Twelve. What to Do When You Have Been Wronged? 138

Chapter Thirteen. Love, the New Commandment 143

Chapter Fourteen. Sickness and Walking Out of Love 153

Chapter Fifteen. Fear of Man 160

Chapter Sixteen. Do Demons Have Legal Rights? 169

Chapter Seventeen. Love is the Key 176

Chapter Eighteen. How to Be Delivered 203

Chapter Nineteen. How to Keep Your Deliverance ... 214

Chapter Twenty. Quotes by Famous People 229

Conclusion 247

Bibliography 249

Introduction

There must be a heightened awareness of the need for deliverance in the body of Christ as well as how to administer this deliverance. This book explores the Holy Bible and what God has to say about deliverance and physical and emotional healing, as well as many years of experience ministering, deliverance, spiritual counseling, and discernment. It also shares numerous testimonies of lives that have been set free. Countless invisible chains that have held people captive and in bondage that have been broken. This book is for different types of people; those that have been held captive by invisible forces and desire to be free, and for those that want to teach others who are held captive to be free. Although this book goes into much detail and real life stories of deliverance, I intend to prove that the number one reason people are in need of deliverance is that the one new commandment that Jesus gave is not obeyed in that person's life, the commandment to love. Love God, love people, and love yourself. There are many that may believe they are okay in that area of their life, their love life, but may find out they really are missing it and may even be causing blocks to your prayers being answered, a block to your healing and even blocking your deliverance. Your spiritual eyes will be opened, and your understanding will be enlightened to the truth and the truth will set you free.

I. People Are Dying for Lack of Knowledge in Deliverance

Although there are many ministers that believe in deliverance and desire to see people free from demonic oppression, there are many more ministers that do not believe in deliverance. There is an ignorance or lack of knowledge in this area within the body of Christ. People are actually perishing because of a lack of knowledge in the area of deliverance and healing.

"Therefore, my people are gone into captivity because they have no knowledge: and their honorable men are famished, and their multitude dried up with thirst" (Isaiah 5:13, KJV).

This subject needs to be taught more in churches and at Christian schools. However, a majority of Christian Universities are not teaching Biblical doctrine concerning this crucial subject of deliverance and healing. And many leaders in the churches today actually deny that deliverance is needed. Therefore, many of these students of the Word have no knowledge in this particular area and are not able to set the captives free nor are they able to mentor other disciples to deliver God's people from bondage. God made His Word and deliverance simple to understand, yet it is strong meat for some. It does belong to God's people that are mature Christians, and the new believers, or babes in Christ, so we must exorcise our senses to discern both good and evil. We need to rightly divide the Word of God and know the many scriptures that we see that Jesus did all throughout His earthly ministry. He told His disciples to go and make disciples of all nations and teach them everything that Jesus had taught them. One of the things that Jesus taught them was to cast out demons and heal the sick. If you consider yourself to be a disciple of Jesus, then you need to know about deliverance and how to walk in it and how to help others walk in freedom from demonic oppression.

II. Deliverance is for Today

Deliverance is one aspect of the ministry of Jesus; God promises in His Word that healing and deliverance are available for His people today. Yet, in most churches a small percentage of God's people are getting healed of their diseases after praying the prayer of faith, fasting, and standing on the Word. People are not getting well from incurable diseases regardless of their denomination, regardless of the church. And it is an attack on the faith of those that believed and trust God. (Wright, *A More Excellent Way*). Many times, people in need of healing are also in need of deliverance.

III. The Effectiveness of Godly Principles

Through this study, on the subject of deliverance and healing, we can see the effectiveness of Godly principles when applied to the lives of the believer. There must be a continuation of renewing the mind with the Word of God. And there must be a relationship between the person that needs deliverance and God based on these insights given and applied.

Administering scriptures, observe and be a doer of the Word. Bring the person back to a relationship with the Father God so He can heal the person from the inside out. The result of the wholeness of spirit is the fruit of physical health, and emotional well-being. (This information, insight, will bring foresight). This information is appropriate not only for those in the fivefold ministry, but all believers to live a life of freedom and will enable Christians to help those around them be free and maintain their freedom as well.

IV. Lack of Love

Further analysis led to the perception that a lack of love is the number one factor in every area where someone is in need of deliverance. There are numerous scriptures, when delved into, will be evident that God requires His people to live a life of love, not only in words, but in thoughts and actions. Scripture shows if we don't abide in the love of God, if we don't love people, or if we don't love ourselves it is an open door for the enemy to have access into lives of people.

It is evident that there are numerous areas where there is a necessity of release from the tormentor and many areas will be discussed here, whether it's spiritually, such as fear, stress, rejection, guilt, bitterness, addictions, oppression, sadness, and or physically, as in diseases, disorders and infirmities, and other bondages as well. Many times when the healing or freedom does not come forth deliverance is required.

Of course, the world, the unsaved, need salvation and deliverance, but there are Christians that are also in need of deliverance. Christians that should be walking in freedom but are in bondage. However, they are looking to the world psychologist and doctors when, in reality, they should be receiving deliverance in the house of God, or through the believers that lead them to the Deliverer.

Jesus is the Deliverer. He came to offer an opportunity to be freed from bondage and from the curse of sin and death. He says in His Word, "If the Son therefore shall make you free, ye shall be free indeed" (John 8:36, KJV).

Jesus defines His purpose for coming to us when He referred to a prophecy of Isaiah. "The Spirit of the Lord is upon Me, because He hath anointed Me to preach the Gospel to the poor, He hath sent Me to heal the broken hearted, to preach deliverance to the captives, and recovering of sight to the blind, to set at liberty them that are bruised" (Luke 4:18, KJV).

CHAPTER ONE

The Invisible Kingdom

Eighty-year-old woman's confession of secrets she kept for many years delivered from depression and sadness.

We had recently made new friends and they asked us to stop by and pray for their friend that was suffering from depression and sadness. When we sat down to pray for her and before she told us anything about herself, other than she was suffering from depression and sadness, I felt led by the Lord to tell her that she needs to forgive herself. And immediately she started crying and confessing something that seemed like she could not wait to release and finally tell someone. She was crying profusely and confessing that many years ago, decades ago, she had an abortion. We helped her to understand that God has forgiven her for that when she repented the first time and asked God to forgive her. Although the abortion of this child was wrong, God is so merciful to forgive us of ALL our sins. God said in John 6:37 that, "...him that cometh to Me I will not cast out." So, we are guaranteed that if we come to Jesus, He will not cast us away. He will receive us, guaranteed!

After counseling her about the abortion and God's love and mercy and just before starting to pray for her she started crying again and said, "I have something else to confess." We were not asking for confessions of past sins, she brought it up. She said, "I cheated on my husband." Now it could have been that she had the abortion because she was not sure whose child it was, but at this point it is not important why she felt she had to do it. We know the thief (the devil) comes to steal, kill, and destroy. It is evident what the enemy was doing at that time in her life, maybe she was feeling unhappy in her marriage or home life, enticing her to have an affair, then became pregnant with a child and the enemy made her feel that she needed to have an abortion. And the enemy tried to destroy many years of her life after that by keeping her in guilt and shame and causing her life to be wasted years of sadness and depression which will also affect other people around you. Jesus came that we would have life and have it in abundance.

I don't believe we are to say to ourselves, *well, we are under grace and we can do whatever we want to do, and God will forgive us*. God warns us in His Word not to do that.

But if we do sin and miss it, He said if we confess our sin, He is faithful and just to forgive us.

She held inside of her this very toxic guilt and shame that was killing her slowly, not allowing her to really live. We shared with her the new commandment that Jesus gave us was to love our neighbor as our self and that means we are to LOVE OURSELVES. Self-hatred is a sin. People that hate, the Bible says, are murders. We led her to forgive herself and release herself from everything that she felt she had done wrong in her life and anything that made her feel guilty and shameful for all these many years.

We don't try to bring up the past history of people. But when we are counseling them and they are upset and crying about the past or angry and hurt about something they themselves have done or someone else did to them it is obvious they need to deal with this now and forgive themselves and others.

We led her to forgive herself, pray and once and for all ask God to forgive her for the abortion and the affair and believe God's Word is true. That she is forgiven, and He will not remember her sin anymore. She does not need to keep remembering the past and bringing it up in her mind over and over. The sin is washed away in the blood of Jesus just like it never happened.

Psalm 32:3,5 Amplified 3, "When I kept silence [before I confessed], my bones wasted away through my groaning all the day long. I acknowledged my sin to You, and my iniquity I did not hide. I said, I will confess my transgressions to the Lord, then you forgave me the guilt and iniquity of my sin."

Holding on to unforgiveness, bitterness, and resentment is an open door to the enemy to have access in our lives. It allows the enemy to have a legal right into our lives. Jesus said, "The prince of this world is coming and he has nothing in Me." I will discuss this in more detail later, but it is possible to have something in us that will be an open door to the enemy to cause us to have psychological and physiological manifestations. This is why many are sick in the church today. These spiritual issues have not been dealt with.

Many problems that people have are fundamentally spiritual with associated physiological and psychological manifestations. We see this in God's Word and through the ministry of Jesus that many people are healed as they are delivered from demonic oppression. This aspect of the ministry of Jesus, healing, and deliverance, was interwoven. Many times, deliverance was needed to receive healing. It was so important that Jesus went from town to town casting out evil spirits and healing all those that were oppressed by the devil. Knowing how to be delivered from bondage is so very important, but it is also vitally important to know how to maintain our freedom once we have been delivered.

It is important to know the root cause that opens the door and allows the enemy access into someone's life. Although there are many reasons for these open doors, it really can be summed up in one category or one word and that word is love, or actually, not walking in nor living a life of love as Jesus commanded us to do.

Open doors to demonic forces are actually a result of not living our lives in obedience to the Word of God. Jesus said that we should love the Lord God with all our heart, mind, and strength and love our neighbor as our self. This sums up the Law and the Prophets. Jesus said, "This new commandment I give unto you, that you love one another, love your neighbor as yourself." Obedience is essential to walking in the freedom that Jesus gave to us.

There is a spiritual battle to fight. Yes, Jesus already won the battle for us and we have the victory through His mighty and powerful death on the cross, burial, and resurrection. Yes, we are free in Christ. Yet, Jesus said the words, "Your adversary the devil." An adversary is an enemy. God makes it clear in His Word that we have an enemy to deal with and we are not to be "ignorant of the devil's devices." Jesus told us to occupy until He returns. The way we fight and keep the doors closed to the enemy, and (demonic forces) off our territory is to obey God's Word.

There is an invisible kingdom. Our enemy exists in the invisible realm. It is vital that we know how our enemy operates and not pretend he does not exist. Because God said that we are not to be ignorant of the devil's devices, we must learn from the Word of God about these warnings concerning Satan, and his tactics. Although he, Satan, and his cohorts are already defeated, but because of his hatred for mankind they desire to continue to put and keep man in bondage. Many people try to blame God for their situation. God is not the source of our problems.

Not that we are to be more focused on Satan and demons, our already defeated foe, but because of the clarity in His Word that we are not to be ignorant of the devil's devices. This signifies that we need to know how our adversary, the devil operates. We cannot or should not ignore the fact that he, Satan, and demons exist. Even though they are in the invisible realm they exist in our world and do attempt to operate, in the lives of the unsaved and the saved, the non-Christians and the Christians.

We know through the Word of God that our battles are not really with people. "We wrestle not against flesh and blood but against principalities, against powers, against rulers of the darkness of this world, against spiritual wickedness in high places (Ephesians 6:12, KJV)." So, there is a wicked kingdom reigning in the heavenlies, which affects the lives of men upon the earth. They are unseen spiritual forces that rule and dominate men who rule seen earthly kingdoms, if men will let them. Men that are dominated and influenced by spiritual rulers in the heavenlies.

There is a kingdom of darkness and the Kingdom of light. In God's great plan of redemption, Jesus came to deliver us from the power and authority of these evil spirits who rule in the realm of darkness.

Giving thanks unto the Father, which hath made us meet to be partakers of the inheritance of the saints in light: Who hath delivered us from the power [authority] of darkness, and hath translated us into the kingdom of his dear Son: in whom we have redemption through his blood, even the forgiveness of sins.
Colossians 1:12-13 (KJV)

Anyone walking in darkness can be dominated by rulers of darkness. These rulers of the darkness also try to rule over believers who are not walking in the light of their redemption, or who don't know or don't exercise their rights and privileges in Christ. If they are not in fellowship with God and walking in the light of His Word. Evil Spirits will dominate believers, if they allow them to, by consent, ignorance, or disobedience to the Word of God.

We, as believers are to take authority over these demons. We are to bind their operation according to the Word of God. "Whatsoever ye shall bind on earth shall be bound in heaven and whatsoever ye shall loose on earth shall be loosed in heaven" (Matthew 18:18, KJV). We are to stand in our authority and bind these classes of evil spirits here on the earth, principalities, powers, and rulers of the darkness of this world. Every unsaved person is in the kingdom of darkness. And they are ruled or motivated by these demons or evil spirits who are the rulers of the darkness of this world.

And you hath he quickened, who were dead in trespasses and sins; wherein in time past ye walked according to the course of this world, according to the prince of the power of the air, the spirit that now worketh in the children of disobedience: among whom also we all had our conversation in times past in the lusts of our flesh, fulfilling the desires of the flesh and of the mind; and were by nature the children of wrath, even as others.
Ephesians 2:1-3 (KJV)

All unrighteousness is sin: and there is a sin not unto death. We know that whosoever is born of God sinneth not; but he that is begotten of God keepeth himself, and that wicked one toucheth him not. And we know that we are of God, and the whole world lieth in wickedness [darkness].
I John 5:19 (KJV)

All wrongdoing is sin, and there is sin which does not [involve] death [that may be repented of and forgiven]. We know [absolutely] that anyone born of God does not [deliberately and knowingly] practice committing sin, but the One Who was begotten of God carefully watches over and protects him [Christ's divine presence within him preserves him against the evil], and the wicked one does not lay hold (get a grip) on him or touch [him]. We know [positively] that we are of God, and the whole world [around us] is under the power of the evil one.

I John 5:17-19 (AMP)

We see from the above scriptures, that God keeps those and protects those that are not living a lifestyle of sin. We are in the world but not of the world. We walk in the light of God's Word and it ensures protection against the evil spirits.

Jesus is our Lord; He is the ruler over us. Satan is the head of those that are unsaved and under his dominion. The spirit world is more real than the physical world. God is a Spirit. Angels exist in the spirit realm and so do evil spirits. Christians have authority over evil spirits, the unsaved do not.

For you are all sons of light and sons of the day; we do not belong either to the night nor to darkness.

I Thessalonians 5:5 (AMP)

"In the beginning was the Word, and the Word was with God, and the Word was God (John 1:1, KJV)." Jesus was and is the Word. Jesus said He is the Light of the world. In John chapter eight just after Jesus told the adulterous woman to go and sin no more, He addressed the crowd and said, "I am the Light of the World. He who follows Me will not walk in the darkness." When we walk in the light, we are a doer of His word.

We are the sons of light and we should walk and be imitators of our Lord Jesus and walk in the light of His Word. His Way, we will walk in love in every area of our lives, our thoughts, our actions, with ourselves, and with others, including those that have hurt us or wronged us in any way.

CHAPTER TWO

Can a Christian Have an Open Door to the Demonic?

Can a Christian be oppressed and have an open door for the enemy to have access into their life? The answer is, yes. Smith Wigglesworth also asked the question, "Is there any place for the enemy in one who has been baptized with the Holy Spirit?" He gave an example of a woman that had been baptized with the Holy Spirit, but years later she became delirious and insane. She became so fascinated with a preacher that would not marry her and the devil had taken advantage of the situation. "Our only safety is in going on with God and constantly being filled with the Holy Spirit. However, before Satan can bring evil spirits there must be an open door (Wigglesworth *Spiritual Gifts*, 123)."

The woman's hope was lost, she allowed herself to listen to the lies of the enemy that she was not loved and was rejected. She allowed herself to lose the peace of God, she concentrated on sad things and by not keeping her mind stayed on the Lord she lost her peace. "If I find my peace is disturbed in any way I know it is the enemy that is trying to work. How do I know this? Because the Lord has promised to keep his mind in perfect peace when it is stayed on Him" Isaiah 26:3. (Wigglesworth *Spiritual Gifts*, 123)."

Paul told us in Romans 12:1 to, "Present our bodies as a living sacrifice, holy acceptable to God, which is our reasonable service." And we would, "Be transformed by the renewing of our mind with the Word of God." Also, God tells us to think on Good things, and things that are pure.

Finally, brethren, whatever things are true, whatever things are noble, whatever things are just, whatever things are pure, whatever things are lovely, whatever things are of a good report, if there is any virtue and if there is anything praiseworthy; meditate on these things.

Philippians 4:8 (KJV)

When people start to meditate on the wrong things, it will open a door to the enemy in the person's life. Everything we do starts with a thought. Good or bad, right, or wrong, everything starts with a thought. If we allow wrong thoughts to enter or remain, a stronghold will develop, solely from wrong thoughts. When in fact we should have, "Cast down every vain imagination and everything that exalts itself against the knowledge of God" (II Cor. 10:5, KJV).

I. HOW CAN A DEMON GET INTO A PERSON?

Have you ever had a home that had termites? They can eat your home and destroy it if you allow them to stay. When a person discovers they have termites in their home, they call a termite exterminator company that will spray the house with something that will get rid of the termites. However, they never ask the homeowner, a person, to also stand there and get sprayed to get rid of the termites. Why? Because the termites were in the house and not in the person that occupied the house. The person did not have the termites in them. The termites were in the house.

You see, we humans are a three part being, spirit, soul, and body. We are a spirit, we have a soul, and we live in a body. Your spirit is the real you. When your time on earth is fulfilled, your spirit will leave your body. Your body will die and go back to the dust. But your spirit is still alive although the body is dead. If you are a Christian, demons cannot have access to your spirit, your spirit is the real you that lives in your body.

Demons try to get access to your body, and your soul (mind, will and emotions) to hinder your walk with the Lord Jesus Christ.

II. OPEN DOOR – EAR GATE

The music we listen to can affect us in wrong ways. If we listen to ungodly songs, they can speak to us with suggestions to sin and eventually believe nothing is wrong with it because after all everyone else is okay with it. Or, *they seem like good people and they are doing the same thing surely it must be okay.* There will be a war of attrition against you, to entice you to sin and you will not even realize that it happened. It can desensitize you.

Allowing negative words that people speak to us or about us to affect us will eventually cause us to have wrong attitudes or negative emotions from rejection and mistreatment by others. We must not allow ourselves to believe the lies that have been spoken over us. Eventually, we can be overcome with these negative emotions until a strongman of resentment, bitterness, and hatred will need to be cast out before freedom will return.

Jesus said, "If you love Me, you will obey Me." That means obedience to the word of God and that means obeying directions about our mind and thought life. We have to be careful what we allow ourselves to meditate on. There are multitudes of people in the world today who are held hostage by the devil in their minds. 1 John 3:8 says, "... For this purpose, the Son of God was manifested, that He might destroy the works of the devil."

II. OPEN DOOR – THOUGHTS/MINDS

The word 'destroy' is taken from the Greek word luo, and it refers to the act of untying or unloosing something. Jesus Christ came into the world to untie, or unloose, Satan's binding power over us.

"How God anointed Jesus of Nazareth with the Holy Ghost and with power, who went about doing good, and healing all that were oppressed of the devil; for God was with Him" (Acts 10:38, KJV) We know from different verses in the Bible that setting people free from Satan's power is a primary concern of Jesus Christ. Since this is His concern, it should be ours as well.

In order to free people from demonic oppression, we must learn how to recognize the work of the enemy and how to overcome his attacks against the mind. The mind is the primary area he seeks to attack. Satan wants to plant a stronghold of deception in some area of an individual's mind. If he is successful, he can then begin to control and manipulate the person.

Woman Angry with Doctor:
We were asked to pray for a woman that had cancerous cyst attached to her female parts. She had been

going to the doctor regularly for checkups and exams, but the doctor found this stage three cancer and she became angry with him that he did not catch it earlier. She became so consumed with negative thoughts about the doctor and his words and the death sentence he pronounced to her; she became bitter toward him. She felt hopelessness, sadness and depression overwhelm her to the point she could barely hold her head up as we were counseling and ministering to her.

The enemy is merciless and is relentless in his attacks. She did not take the thoughts captive as the enemy was presenting them to her. If we do not cast down the thoughts immediately, and we agree with the enemy and have thoughts or something against someone, it will create a hole in our spiritual armor that protects us against the enemy. God said, "Don't let the sun go down on your wrath, it will give place to the devil."

When we engage in spiritual warfare, we must always proceed with the Word of God as our guide and foundation. It is more than just dealing with the devil. We must understand that there are other elements of spiritual warfare that are also vital such as taking control of our minds and crucifying the flesh.

There is power in living a crucified life and the devil's attacks against our lives would not work if our flesh did not cooperate. If we live our lives "dead to sin," (Romans 6:2) we would not respond to demonic suggestion and to fleshly temptation. Living the crucified life is a critical part of spiritual warfare.

A person can scream at the devil all day long, but if that person has willfully permitted some area of his mind to go unchecked and unguarded, if he is aware of an area of sin but has not been willing to deal with it, he has opened the door for an attack on himself. In that case, all his prayers against the devil will be to no avail because his real enemy is not the devil. Rather, his own carnal mind and flesh which must be submitted to the control of the Holy Spirit in order to eradicate these attacks (Renner *Dressed To Kill*, 22).

2 Corinthians 10:3-5 denotes mental bondages that must be pulled down:

For though we walk (live) in the flesh, we are not carrying on our warfare according to the flesh and using mere human weapons. For the weapons of our warfare are not physical [weapons of flesh and blood], but they are mighty before God for the overthrow and destruction of strongholds, [Inasmuch as we] refute arguments and theories and reasonings and every proud and lofty thing that sets itself up against the [true] knowledge of God; and we lead every thought and purpose away captive into the obedience of Christ (the Messiah, the Anointed One).

Although these bondages and strongholds in the mind may have attached themselves to us in the past when we were still under Satan's control. In context, these verses are referring to a person making a decision to take charge of his mind and take the thoughts of his mind captive. And First Peter 2:11 says, "Beloved, I implore you as aliens and strangers and exiles [in this world] to abstain from the sensual urges (the evil desires, the passions of the flesh, your lower nature) that wage war against the soul." This describes the flesh warring against the soul or the flesh attempting to conquer and subdue the mind (Renner *Dressed to Kill*, 41).

We must keep our minds and our flesh under the control of the Holy Spirit. Every thought captive to the obedience of Christ, to obey is better than sacrifice. He has commanded us to love, love in our actions, love in our words, and love in our thoughts.

Most believers who have fallen in recent times, would not have fallen if they had not given the devil a foothold in their minds. They have left a door open for a demonic attack somewhere along the way by not dealing with an unseen, private area of their lives.

Demon spirits have absolutely no power to bring about destruction unless they can find an open door into a person's mind, then they can begin to introduce evil influences and launch their attacks upon the individual.

The Holy Spirit is faithful to convict us of any areas in our lives that leave us vulnerable to attack. He will urge us to repent and change before the devil builds strongholds in our thinking. However, it is still up to us to see that these opened doors are slammed shut and forever closed. But if we ignore the Holy Spirit's pleading and we allow sin, willfully permitted temptation, or wrong attitudes to persist in our lives, unconfessed and unchanged we are leaving gaping holes through which the enemy will seek to undo us. Most spiritual destruction is avoidable, but only if we will reverently listen to the pleading of the Holy Spirit and obey His warnings to us. Demon spirits cannot destroy without an open door into a person's soul, and such an entrance can only be given by way of permission.

Evil forces may try to hinder us, but they cannot destroy someone unless there is something already wrong in us to which they can use for destruction. (Paul's personal consecration to the Lord was his greatest defense against the enemy).

I have prayed for many people that needed deliverance and many have been gloriously set free by the power of God. However, there have been times that some people were set free in some areas of their life but still had some issues that seemed as if they were not free in certain areas. People tend to look for cure-all solutions that do not make them look at their own flaws or deal with their flesh. This is often why they flock to teachings and methods that offer relatively simple solutions to lifelong problems. Holding fast to God's Word and applying its principles to their lives seems to take too long and will be more difficult to do. After all, the Word of God requires a person to live a crucified life. It demands that he repent of a wrong thought life. It insists that he seek to conform to the image of Jesus Christ.

Therefore, the thought of an instant cure is very alluring, to the uncommitted and spiritually immature who are looking for a "quick fix" to change their deeply rooted, habitual, and often self-imposed problems (Renner *Dressed To Kill*, 55). Before we came to the Lord Jesus Christ, we had no eternal perspective and no constant biblical standard to live by. (Renner, *Dressed to Kill*, 87)

Free, Yet Still Bound?

A pastor that I know from Kenya, Africa described how the goats are tied up in Africa but once they are untied, the goat believes he is still bound and will continue to lie on the ground after he has been set free. In the goats mind, he believes he is still bound by the ropes and will continue to lie on the ground and remain in mental bondage even though he has been set free.

Christians also were previously bound by Satan's destructive power then we received Jesus Christ as our Lord and Savior and were born again and free from Satan's kingdom of darkness. However, often we don't perceive that we have been freed. Many people are still bound up in scars, pains, and mental hang-ups, not realizing that they have really been set free. We are free, but we must maintain our Christ-bought, Christ-imparted freedom by renewing our minds. Freedom becomes a way of life only as we replace our wrong thinking and wrong believing with what the Word of God declares about our new condition.

Those that have just been saved often times must work to overcome the emotional and mental scars they received when they were still in the world under the devil's control. Although the inner man has been born again and made new, the mind and the body must still be conformed to the image of the inner man. These newly saved individuals may have received much abuse while they were still held captive by the consequences of sin. Perhaps they struggled with a bad marriage, sexual perversion, a lying spirit, mental hang-up, rejection, abandonment, or some other type of scar that was inflicted on their souls before they met the Lord.

If these areas from the past are not removed through the renewing of the mind by the Word of God, these strongholds can and will continue to exert power in the life of a Christian. Moreover, if these "residual areas" are not dealt with according to the Word, they are the very areas that Satan will use to wage warfare against that person's new life.

When the adversary locates an area in our lives that has never been surrendered to the sanctifying work of the Holy Spirit, he will try to seize that un-surrendered area in our minds and use that stronghold to work against the growth and development of our new freedom in Jesus Christ. This is why our refusal to deal with specific areas of sin in our lives is where the majority of spiritual warfare stems from.

Satan needs an open door to gain access into our lives. Some examples would be memories of terrible experiences that happened before we knew the Lord that we still allow to dominate our emotions. Or fears that were transferred to us from our parents, family members, or friends. With these as well as others, the mind is the strategic center where the warfare with the "god of the world" takes place. (Renner *Dressed to Kill*, 106).

CHAPTER THREE

Open Doors to the Demonic

I. CHOICES & CONSEQUENCES

God loves us so much that He gave each person a free will to choose between right and wrong, to do good or evil, life or death, blessing or cursing. He told us to, "choose life" but ultimately, we will decide our future by our choices that we make now. Wrong choices that lead us into sin, and all wrongdoing is sin, is an open door to demonic forces in our life.

Since sin, is anything contrary to the Word of God, it is evident that it would be in opposition to the New Commandment that Jesus gave us, to love the Lord God with all our heart, soul, mind and strength, and love our neighbor as our self. This new commandment to love, Jesus said, "Sums up all the law and the prophets." This means all previous laws, precepts, and ordinances. Every law that was ever given in Old Testament.

We are commanded to love God, love people, and love our self. If we miss it in these areas, it can allow open doors to the demonic in our lives.

We all have crossroads in our lives - moments in time in which God speaks to our hearts, and we choose either to stand by the Word of the Lord or to go our own way, to live a life of love or a life void of it. These crossroads can seem great or small but none of them lacks significance. <u>Our lives today are nothing more than the result of the decisions we made yesterday and all our previous days.</u>

You are the "control center" of your life. Satan desires to gain control of your soul because that's where he can influence your will, the part of you that makes choices. (Renner *Dream Thief*, 233). However, it is crucial to note that Satan can't force you to do anything! You are the final authority when it comes to what you choose to believe, the attitudes you choose to develop, to choose to love or not to love, to choose to forgive or not forgive. Ultimately, you decide whether or not you do what God wants you to do, or, you will do things your way, or Gods way. That's why Romans 12:2 is so important. You should continuously "...be transformed by the renewing of your mind, that ye may prove what is that good, and acceptable, and perfect, will of God." His will is that we love unconditionally.

God exhorts us again and again to keep our minds renewed, washed, and sharpened by studying and meditating on His Word. Staying in God's Word is essential to walking in the spirit and not in the flesh and to discern between good and evil in the realm of the senses.

Abiding continually in the Word builds our understanding and establishes the spiritual foundation in our lives. Spiritual truths to love, the power of the Word, and the power of love, the power to be free in Christ and the power to maintain our freedom by having the love of God on the inside of us and stirring it up with acts of love, mercy and kindness even to those that have hurt us, wronged us or may have previously wounded us. It gives us supernatural strength and courage to be a 'doer' of the Word and not a 'hearer' only. To love those who do not love us. To bless those that persecute us and do us wrong. It enables us to come into divine alignment with the Word of God. Faith and love will flourish in our lives because we choose them over our flesh and the deceptive practices of the devil if we don't abide in God's Word.

If you abide in My Word [continually obeying my teachings and living in accordance with them, then] you are truly My disciples. And you will know the truth and the truth will set you free [from the penalty of sin].
                                    John 8:31-32 (AMP)

His Word is true. His Word teaches us to love one another. The truth will set you free, in other words, you will not be bound and in need of deliverance. The truth will set us free. Love will set us free. God is love. Perfect love: "cast out" fear, and anything that would try to keep us bound.

The true power in every one of our lives lies in our own will. Every day of our lives we have to make choices. We can choose to do things our own way, choose not to love, choose not to walk in peace, choose not to forgive, choose to have resentment, and bitterness. However, when we choose to go our own way, and not love it is ultimately inspired and directed by Satan. Or we can choose to love everyone and forgive anyone for anything which is always inspired and directed by the Word and the Holy Spirit.

Many times, when we make the right choice to love someone that has hurt us or wronged us it may seem insignificant, or difficult, and even seem impossible, but the Word of God declares that if we love God, we will obey Him, and that means choose to be obedient to love God, love people, and love ourselves. We will have clean hands, a pure heart, pure thoughts and will close the door to the enemy and he will not have access into our lives.

Open Doors to the Demonic

The devil and his kingdom are using TV and movies to deceive people, disobey God's Word, and open the doors to the demonic in people's lives. They are led to believe in so many lies of the enemy, from psychics to haunted houses. I have heard people say they have watched psychics on TV, and they believed them too, because the psychic knew so much about a dead relative and it was impossible for anyone else to have known, so it must be real. Alleged contact with the dead is called necromancy and is forbidden by the Lord in the Law. "Give no regard to mediums and familiar spirits, do not seek after them, to be defiled by them: I am the Lord your God". (Leviticus 19:31, KJV).

Also:

There shall not be found among you anyone that taketh his son or his daughter to pass through the fire, or that useth divination, or an observer of times, or and enchanter, or a witch, or a charmer, or a consulter with familiar spirits, or a wizard, or a necromancer, for all who do these things are an abomination to the Lord.

Deuteronomy 18:10-12 (KJV)

These psychics are actually getting their information from a familiar spirit. A familiar spirit is a demonic spirit that has become familiar with people, places, and events that have occurred in a specific location. These types of spirits desire to remain in the area where they originated or where they have controlled individuals throughout the history in that region. For example, when Christ expelled the demons from the tombs, the spirits request that Christ not send them out of the country. (Mark 5:10). The spirit world is real. These are not spirits of the departed, but of demonic entities that have existed since the fall of Satan. Any past information can be revealed to a medium who channels evil spirits. (Stone, Satan's Playbook 148). There are also popular "Reality" television shows of people that are hunting ghost or spirits of the dead that are haunting houses. However, the truth is they are nothing more than a roaming demonic entity. The biblical truth is that once a person dies, that person's spirit will immediately depart and immediately abide in one of two places, whether paradise in the third heaven (2 Corinthians 12:1-4) or hell (Luke 16).

"This generation is obsessed with the paranormal, but it must be taught the supernatural from a biblical perspective. Often, pastors must spend their time ministering words of encouragement to their members from Sunday to Sunday and are not always aware of the paranormal culture brewing in around them and of the desire for this generation to understand the world around them and of the desire for this generation to understand the world of angels and spirits. This hunger must be met with biblical warnings related to occult practices and biblical knowledge of the spirit world and its operation" (Stone, Satan's Playbook, 152).

Parents are allowing their children to watch Harry Potter movies. Harry is a wizard. Nothing else needs to be said in a Christian family about the decision to give permission to their children to watch such demonic movies. In fact, many parents encourage the reading of Harry Potter books because they say it increases the reading skill of the child. I actually knew of a child that told me that the school they were attending was offering extra credit if they would read Harry Potter books and they were giving them away at some book bus. Thank God she heard a message about deliverance and the dangers of these Harry Potter books and movies and did not receive the book that was offered to her based on what she learned in church. Wizards and the like are an abomination unto God and is nothing to be played with or taken lightly. Again, if we love God and obey His commandments, we will not allow such things in our homes or have any place in our lives.

We need to have more pastors teaching about God's Word that He is warning the body of Christ against these abominations. Jesus is coming back for His bride without spot or wrinkle.

CHAPTER FOUR

The Strong Man

Jesus said that, "If I, with the finger of God cast out devils, no doubt the kingdom of God is come upon you" (Luke 11:19, KJV). There is an invisible kingdom that is behind strongholds and bondages, so we must learn how to be free and help others to be free.

And if I by Beelzebub cast out devils, by whom do your sons cast them out? Therefore, shall they be your judges. But if I, with the finger of God, cast out devils, no doubt the kingdom of God is come upon you. When a strong man armed keeps his palace, his goods are in peace. But when a stronger than he shall come upon him, and overcome him, he taketh from him all his armor wherein he trusted, and divideth his spoils. He that is not with Me is against Me: and He that gathers not with Me scattereth. When the unclean spirit is gone out of a man, he walks through dry places, seeking rest; and finding none, he saith I will return unto my house whence I came out and when he cometh he finds it swept and garnished. Then goeth he and taketh to him seven other spirits more wicked than himself; and they enter and dwell there: and the last state of that man is worse than the first.

Luke 11:19-26 (KJV)

This is talking about some type of individual who is strong, who is armed, and who is in control of his house or his palace. 'So, thereby his goods are protected.' This is a statement of Satan's control over a human by a kingdom.

The "palace" is a human being. The strongman is the principality that is controlling that human's life then returns bringing seven other spirits stronger that reinforce its power in that life. There are things in a person's life that allows the strongman to remain and he does not have to leave until they are removed. For example, the strong man of bitterness cannot be removed until a person gets rid of unforgiveness. Unforgiveness gives bitterness power. Other things may have to be removed first such as resentment, retaliation, rage, hatred, violence, murder, that are fueling the strongman's power. These elements are the flesh and action of Satan's kingdom in a human, give the power to the strongman called Bitterness (Wright, *Addictions* 32).

If someone wants to get rid of bitterness but cannot because the strongman of Bitterness is trusting in the fact that the entire power structure that gives him authority in the person's life is intact, but God wants it to be removed. The context of what Jesus is teaching in these scriptures is the reality of evil spirits working in humans. When an evil spirit is cast out, it wanders through a dry place, seeking a place of rest because it is in torment. When it is cast out, the human is at peace, and the spirit is in torment.

In unraveling spiritual issues, we have to dismantle that armor that gives that strong man the power to rule. For example;

> *"The strong Man in addictions is an unloving, unclean spirit. These spirits will not let you accept God's love, will not let you be at peace with yourself in the new birth, and will not let you give and receive love from others the way you need to. What feeds it has to be dismantled. It is not just a matter of conversion; it is a matter of restructuring your entire spiritual personality by removing the armor that has become part of our lives spiritually and psychologically."*
> (Wright, *Addictions*, 36)

In Luke chapter eleven, after Jesus delivered a man from demons, He continues to say in verse 28, "Blessed (happy to be envied) rather are those who hear the Word of God and obey and practice it!" It is so very important to remain delivered, a person must be obedient to the

Word of God. Otherwise, sin will cause the strongman to remain in the house (or person).

There must be true repentance for any sin issues in the delivered person. Otherwise, the sin remains and thereby enhancing the armor of the strongman. It is not just a sin issue. It is a spiritual root issue that produces the sin. "We ostracize people in certain sexual sins because we do not understand the root problems that lie behind the sexual addiction. The same thing that is behind sexual addiction is the same thing that is behind drug addiction, alcoholism, and prescription drug abuse. It is the same thing: the need to be loved, drives them to find an altered state of consciousness." (Wright, *Addictions*, 40)

Things like pride, arrogance, guilt, self-hatred, shame, self-pity are also part of the armor of Luke Chapter eleven. This is the stuff the strongman is counting on to keep in place in the person's life, so you cannot overthrow him, and he controls them in their need to be loved.

There is a kingdom setup to bind you. You alone choose your freedom or your bondage. We must quit blaming others for our feelings, circumstances, et. God has given us the ability to choose so we must understand how to defeat the strong man behind the spiritual issues. It involves, recognition, taking responsibility, repentance and taking a stand. Allowing these spiritual issues to take over our lives is not letting God be Lord over our life.

"All I can do is take you to His presence and His Word and a conviction of the Holy Spirit. In ministry, we begin to methodically remove the armor that gives power to the strongman. We begin to show God's love, and we begin to bring the person to a place where he can start to believe that he is loved. Perfect love cast out fear." (Wright, *Addictions*, 52)

There is no fear in love; but perfect love casteth out fear: because fear hath torment. He that feareth is not made perfect in love.

1 John 4:18 (KJV)

Some of the armor that needs to be stripped in order to produce freedom from the strongman: Cruelty, rage, verbal abuse, retaliation, self-hatred, violence, slander, malice, gossip, sleeplessness, nervous stomach, nervousness, headaches, red eyes, physical illness, poor eating habits, nervous breakdown, cirrhosis of the liver, anxiety, fear of being rejected, paranoia, fear of failure, resentment, fear of being unwanted, guilt, insecurity, self-hatred, intimidation, hopelessness, hatred of others, inability to give or receive love freely (1 John 4:18), impairment of judgment, indecision, shame, condemnation, depression, inability to communicate, slow thinking feelings of worthlessness, despair, sorrow, emptiness, no hope, jealousy, madness, despair, and torment.

But there is hope. The love of God gives you the ability to defeat a strongman. We must accept our sonship, learn to love God, receive His love, and know that we are loved. Then God will put a love in your heart for others that will remain.

The ability to give love and the ability to receive love keeps me from spiritual issues and strongholds, preserves us in the sanctity of our marriages, keeps us from pornography, keeps us out of adultery, and keeps us safe. No torment, just peace. We will no longer be spiritually bewitched, no longer bound by the sorcerer and the unclean spirits. That is the fruit of the gospel! (Wright, *Addictions*, 56)

However, there are many people that know the Word of God yet continue to do the things that are not pleasing to God and are against His Word. Verse 32 of Luke chapter eleven reads, "The men of Nineveh will appear as witnesses at the judgment with this generation and will condemn it; for they repented at the preaching of Jonah, and behold, here is more than Jonah." Jesus is greater than Jonah. We have Jesus, His Word, and even more than Jonah, today we have the Holy Spirit living in us, leading us, guiding us. The Holy Spirit is the umpire of our soul (Colossians 3:13). When we get those promptings from the Holy Spirit to do or not do something and a person goes against those leadings and sins anyway these sins are open doors to the demonic or strongman and create these strongholds.

Jesus said, "No one after lighting a lamp puts it in a cellar or crypt or under a bushel measure, but on a lamp stand, that those who are coming in may see the light. Your eye is the lamp of your body; when your eye (your conscience) is sound *and* fulfilling its office, your whole body is full of light; but when it is not sound and is not fulfilling its office, your body is full of darkness. Verse 35 of Luke Chapter eleven reads, "Be careful, therefore, that the light that is in you is not darkness." If then your entire body is illuminated, having no part dark, it will be wholly bright [with light], as when a lamp with its bright rays gives you light.

Jesus said be careful that there is no darkness in you. He warns us about what is on the inside of us and that we are not to be outwardly religious yet neglect to keep our inside or our hearts clean by things such as stealing, having greed, spitefulness, hatred, bitterness, rancor, gossip, being ungodly or immorality and so much more. Verse 39, "But the Lord said to him, 'Now you Pharisees cleanse the outside of the cup and of the plate, but inside you yourselves are full of greed and robbery *and* extortion *and* malice *and* wickedness.'"

Jesus in the very next few verses talked about our inward righteousness makes us purified and clean. Yes, we are cleansed by the blood of Jesus when we are born again, but if we willfully, deliberately, continue to sin without repentance we are acting as unrighteous. "You senseless (foolish, stupid) ones [acting without reflection or intelligence]! Did not He Who made the outside make the inside also? But [dedicate your inner self and] give as donations to the poor of those things which are within [of inward righteousness] and behold, everything is purified *and* clean for you. But woe to you, Pharisees! For you tithe mint and rue and every [little] herb, but disregard *and* neglect justice and the love of God. These you ought to have done without leaving the others undone."

Again, we see Jesus talking about love in the Word of God. Having the love of God on the inside of us is the opposite of the things Jesus mentioned that would make us unclean on the inside such as greed, robbery, malice, and wickedness. When we love our brother, we will not steal from him; we will not wish ill will toward our brother, we will love and not hate our brother whom we have seen.

God sees the integrity of our heart. When we come before God, He knows if there is unforgiveness, resentment, bitterness or any sin that may be hidden from man, but God sees the heart or our spirit. He knows if we have true repentance.

If you want to make sure your heart is right with God (and you should want to) in every area of your life, ask God to shine His spotlight inside of you and reveal to you any area in your life where you may need to make changes. Ask Him if there is anything that is not pleasing to Him. It could be something you think is a little insignificant thing such as wrong attitudes, but those little things are important to God. And God knows those things you may consider small matters, or little sins, will be an open door to the enemy in your life.

God loves you with unconditional love and He wants you to live a victorious life. In order to walk in the victory that Jesus paid the price for, we must keep ourselves free from the snares or the traps of the enemy. If you sense a conviction that there is an area of your life that needs to change, repent of it. Ask God to forgive you and then let it go, don't keep dwelling on past mistakes or sins. Know that God loves you and you are forgiven. You are greatly loved.

CHAPTER FIVE

Bitterness is a Principality

The number one objective assigned by Satan, is to keep you from knowing Christ as a Savior. But if he fails in that, his objective is to keep you (Christians) from serving Christ effectively. He does that by going against what God wants you to do. We know that the new commandment that Jesus gave us was to love the Lord God with all our heart, soul, mind, and strength and to love our neighbor as our self. So that is the area that the enemy is looking to make you fall. He will try to destroy the love in you. He wants to destroy your love for others, and even loving yourself. If you sin in the area of your love walk and begin to feel hurt and then the bitterness and resentment sets in it gives him a legal right into your life. This is why God said, "Be angry and sin not: let not the sun go down upon your wrath: neither give place to the devil" (Ephesians 4:26, KJV). So, God is telling us very clearly here that if we continue to be angry it will give a place to the devil in our lives. We need to be quick to forgive. Let it go. Often, people allow a root of bitterness to enter and grow in their hearts and then deliverance is needed to be free from this spirit of bitterness.

Pastor Daniel Ekechukwu is a man from Nigeria that was raised from the dead at a Rhinehard Bonnke crusade. He came here to the USA to minister at the River Church in Tampa, Florida and I was so blessed to hear him preach. He preached powerfully with the fire of God as he warned the people that when he actually died, he was going to go to hell because he had unforgiveness in him toward his wife. He said that he did not have on the Breastplate of Righteousness. He was not in right standing with God concerning forgiveness. He was on his way to hell and although he was a pastor, angels were talking to him telling him the reason he was going to hell was because of he did not forgive his wife. During this time, he could see that thousands of people were being sent to hell. Sowing and reaping what you sow: If you sow unforgiveness, then God cannot forgive you. You cannot sow unforgiveness to someone and reap forgiveness from God. Those who die with unforgiveness go to hell, Matthew 6:14, "If you don't forgive, neither will your Heavenly Father forgive you."

Those who live with unforgiveness are delivered over to tormenting spirits if they do not repent. We find this in the scriptures, about the unforgiving servant. He was called wicked by his Lord; when he would not forgive, he was turned over to the tormentors (Matthew 18:32). It is a matter of the heart.

The devil will put thoughts in your mind, *Hey you have Bible studies, you have a church, or you have led many people to the Lord, you are ok or you've been attending church for twenty years, surely the Lord will overlook this.* The victim buys into the lie not knowing it is the devil.

Use the sword of the Spirit which is the Word of God. Mark 11:25, When you pray if you have anything against anyone you must forgive. There are people in Hell that are yelling out that "I thought I had more time!" to get right with God. You may not have any remorse now but later it will be too late; it will be too late!

Jesus said if someone sins against you seven times you must forgive. Later Peter asked Jesus, "How many times?" Maybe he must have felt like he had enough of someone and was double checking if their number was up and he could hold something against them. Jesus said we must forgive. Jesus also said if a brother sins against you go and tell him so. If he continues, bring a witness; then if he continues bring it before the church and let him be to you as a publican and a sinner. (If they really repent that means they will stop sinning against you.)

The Holy Spirit will lead us in various ways as we minister to people.

Jesus said:

The Spirit of the Lord is upon me, because He hath anointed Me to preach the Gospel to the poor; He hath sent me to heal the brokenhearted, to preach deliverance to the captives, and recovering of sight to the blind, to set at liberty them that are bruised, to preach the acceptable year of the Lord. And He closed the book, and He gave it again to the minister and sat down. And the eyes of all them that were in the synagogue were fastened on him. And He began to say unto them, this day is this scripture fulfilled in your ears.

Luke 4:18 (KJV)

How God anointed Jesus of Nazareth with the Holy Ghost and with power: who went about doing good and healing all that were oppressed of the devil; for God was with Him.

Acts 10:38 (KJV)

After this, Jesus went to the Cross and paid the price for our sins. He suffered for us and He said that when we take communion do it in remembrance of Him. WE REMEMBER the stripes and beating He took on His back. The crown of thorns that was put on His head. We remember, the nails that were driven into his hands left and right, we remember the nails that were pounded into His feet. We remember the sword that pierced His side. We are to remember and know that He did that for us. His blood was poured out for us. He paid the price for our sins. How great is the love that God has for us? When we receive Him as our Lord and Savior and we receive the seal of the Holy Spirit on us. He won the victory over the enemy for us.

God said in His word that He gives us authority over the enemy. If someone is on your property, police have power and authority in the name of the law to go into areas, places where people are causing problems and chaos to stop and get the people off of your property that are trying to wrong you. God has given us power and authority over the enemy in our own lives. The power of God and the name of Jesus. In the name of Jesus, the enemy of your soul must go. We need to recognize and know when the enemy is at work in our lives and how he gets legal authority in our lives, how to get rid of any demonic forces that may have had an open door to oppress you.

Of course, we need to distinguish if we are really dealing with demons or is it the flesh. The flesh being the old carnal nature, or the old man. Demons being persons moving in and occupy areas of your personality.

An example to compare the two: Flesh is carcass and vultures are demons. Jesus said, "where the carcass is the vultures will be gathered." Where the unregenerate flesh of man is exposed in its carnality and sinfulness you can be sure the demons will be gathered there.

The remedies are totally different for the flesh and demons. The remedy for the flesh is the cross. Galatians 5:24, "They that are Christ have crucified the flesh and its lust. Remedies for demons are to expel them."

It is important to know that demons do not occupy a Christian's spirit. We are a spirit and our spirit lives in our body, and we have a soul. We are three part being, spirit, soul, and body. When the enemy, a demonic spirit comes, God's Word says in Ephesians 6:11 that we should, "Put on the whole armor of God that we may be able to stand against the strategies and the deceits of the devil." Ephesians 6:13-18, "Therefore, put on God's complete armor, that you may be able to resist and stand your ground on the evil day,...., belt of truth around your loins, breastplate of righteousness, right standing with God, feet preparation [to face the enemy with] with the Gospel of peace. Lift up over all the [covering] shield of faith, upon which you can quench all the flaming missiles of the wicked one. Take the helmet of salvation and the sword that the Spirit wields, which is the Word of God. Pray at all times in the Spirit, ...Keep alert and watch with strong purpose and perseverance, interceding in behalf of all the saints."

The armor of God does not include something to cover our backside. God did not expect us to turn and run from the enemy. The Glory of The Lord is our rear guard!

> *His fame went throughout all of Syria and they brought unto Him all who were sick, people with diseases and torments, devils, palsy, and He healed them.*
>
> Matthew 4:24 (KJV)

> *So the report of Him spread throughout all Syria, and they brought Him all who were sick, those afflicted with various diseases and torments, those under the power of demons, and epileptics, and paralyzed people, and He healed them.*
>
> Matthew 4:24 (AMP)
>
> *Who forgives all your sins, who heals all your diseases?*
>
> Psalms 103:3 (KJV)

> *If we judge ourselves, we should not be judged.*
>
> I Corinthians 11:31 (KJV)

Healing and deliverance come as a direct result of sanctification. You can't have your blessings and keep your sins.

The Lord is not putting evil on us, but giving us over to the devices of our own heart until we have had enough. When we recognize the spiritual defects of our life through conviction by the Holy Spirit and through the washing of the Word, the spiritual defect is then purified. Some call it the "Baptism of Fire" – the purging work, the sanctifying work of the Holy Spirit.

There are different types of sickness and disease, some are common to man and some are from demonic oppression. We have the Commandment to love God with all our heart, soul, mind, and strength and love our neighbor as our self. We are Commanded to love God, love people and love ourselves.

Many people do not like themselves and have self-hatred, lack of self-esteem, and guilt. How can you not love yourself if God loves you? He's greater than you are. He who is greatest and holiest of all, God the Father, says He loves you. If we do not love ourselves, we are in opposition to God. We deny His statement of love and open ourselves up to the enemy to agree with us. So, instead of hearing God speaking to you by His Word and by the Holy Spirit, telling you that you are loved, and you are okay, you are going to hear this voice coming into your mind, telling you how terrible, unwanted or worthless you are.

There are many autoimmune diseases: Lupus, Chrohns, diabetes (type 1), rheumatoid arthritis and MS, to name a few. Autoimmune diseases have a spiritual root of self-hated, self-bitterness and guilt. Diabetes and all diseases can be defeated. They can be defeated or can be prevented (Wright, *More Excellent Way*, 227).

When someone says, "This is incurable; they are just going to die anyway." This means that the person believes Satan and death are greater than God and the Lord Jesus and His Word.

A sound heart is the life of the flesh: but envy the rottenness of the bones. (non-menopausal osteoporosis). Envy and jealousy are the cause of rotting of the bones (Proverbs 14:30, KJV).

A merry heart doeth good like a medicine: but a broken spirit drieth the bones (Proverbs 17:22, KJV). Laughter can strengthen the immune system. (The immune system is in the bones).

"Did someone break your heart? People are damaged on the inside so severely they have a compromised immune system." According to Dr. Henry Wright, "Allergies, et. Are just a by-product"

Example: Environmental Illness

The immune system can become compromised because of fear and anxiety coming out of a broken heart. When you have a compromised immune system, you automatically have allergies.

When Christ died it was for all the sins of the world. When Jesus died, He said, "It is finished." Why isn't everyone saved? Because you have to appropriate it by faith. It is the same way with healing. When it says, "By

His stripes we were healed, and He bore the penalty of the curse" (Isaiah 53:5, KJV).

If we are totally free at conversion, then why would we need to be sanctified? Paul tells us about circumcision of the heart. Paul says to cleanse ourselves from all filthiness of the flesh and spirit.

Having therefore these promises, dearly beloved, let us cleanse ourselves from all filthiness of the flesh and spirit, perfecting holiness in the fear of God.

II Corinthians 7:1 (KJV)

Appropriating His grace and mercy in His Word and by the circumcision of our heart and is an ongoing process. God is continually cutting away of the nature He did not create from the beginning.

God's principles of righteousness have never changed. "For I am the Lord, I change not" (Malachi 3:6, KJV).

WE ARE TO LOVE OTHERS: (Love Our Neighbor as Our Self)

Bitterness is a principality of the enemy.

For we wrestle not against flesh and blood, but against principalities, against powers, against the rulers of the darkness of this world, against spiritual wickedness in high places.

Ephesians 6:12 (KJV)

If we are in conflict with one another, I am not your enemy. You are not my enemy. The problem is we are not able to separate the person from their sin. Their sin is our enemy – NOT THEM!

When someone violates us, we make him or her evil along with the evil they did. You have to be able to separate people from their sin. God didn't create you from the foundation of the world as a sinner. He created you from the beginning as saints before Him and as His sons and daughters forever.

Because of sin, we have become separated from Him. Even after conversion, we still have many things to work out. We need to stop being sinning saints.

BITTERNESS

Bitterness is a principality; and there are other spirits that reinforce bitterness.

1. Unforgiveness: If you allow a root of bitterness to get foothold, the first thing that happens is a record of wrongs. "Looking diligently lest any man fail of the grace of God; lest any root of bitterness springing up trouble you, and thereby many be defiled" (Hebrews 12:15, KJV). Wow! God said we become defiled when we have bitterness. (Dictionary.com defines the word defiled as, to make foul, dirty, or unclean; pollute; taint; debase. Other words related to defile are spoilt, dishonored, polluted, and impure).

If you are having flashbacks about things done against you and have a list of reasons why you don't like someone. This is unforgiveness. After unforgiveness gets a foothold and it creates a record of wrongs, there is another dimension of the spiritual dynamics called resentment.

2. <u>Resentment</u>: Is the record of wrongs being fueled by feelings of holding onto it and starting to meditate it. (This is where the enemy really starts working overtime in your thoughts and in your mind; the devil's playground.)

3. <u>Retaliation</u>: Then you have retaliation. Did you ever hear anyone say, "I don't forgive, I just get even." Or maybe you find yourself trying to find ways to get back at the person who wronged you. Retaliation wants to make the person pay for what they have done. It will make you feel like it's time to get even.

4. <u>Anger</u>: After retaliation gets a foothold then anger starts to set in. Unforgiveness, resentment, and retaliation have been building and now a real strong feeling of anger comes along.

5. <u>Hatred</u>: Is the next step after anger.

6. <u>Violence</u>: After hatred comes violence. Violence really starts speaking and says, "You are going to know my pain."

7. <u>Murder</u>: The final fruit of bitterness is murder. Oh, how the Bible warns us against hatred and bitter-

ness. He tells us in advance that anyone who hates his brother is a murderer. What God expects of us is to forgive 70 x 7 in a day.

To forgive, you do not have to condone their sin, but you do have to love them. If you refuse to obey God's Word, and refuse to love the one that wronged you, there will be an open door to the enemy. Once this door is open in your life, if you do not repent and forgive the person and command the demon spirit to leave you in the name of Jesus, the enemy can bring with him seven more spirits and your condition will be worse than the first. It has been said that unforgiveness is like you taking rat poison and waiting for the rat to die. It only hurts you when you are bitter. Love and Forgiveness will set you free from these tormenting spirits.

CHAPTER SIX

Unholy Thoughts

Asian Gentleman Delivered from Suicidal Thoughts, Lust, Anger and Pornography:
We received a call from someone, a lady from Thailand, that was crying out for help for a friend of hers that was playing Russian Roulette. He was struggling in his marriage, addicted to pornography, and had anger issues. We agreed to meet with him and pray with him. Before we prayed of course, we inquired about what was happing in his life and asked him what he personally feels he needs prayer for and make sure he is ready to submit entirely to God and give up all sin because the only way to be truly free and stay free is to first submit to God then you can resist the devil and he will flee.

Submit yourselves therefore to God. Resist the devil, and he will flee from you.

James 4:7 (KJV)

Before you can resist the devil, you must first submit to God. What does that mean, to submit to God? That means obey His teachings, His promptings, His leading, His voice, His direction for our lives. So, we must make a decision to be obedient in every area including our thought life. People must be honest and repentant, and of a contrite heart, ready to be delivered.

We were praying for him and everything seemed fine UNTIL I sensed in my spirit to ask him the question, "Have you ever been involved in an abortion?" After I asked the question, he immediately jumped up and went into a major demonic manifestation. He turned EXTREMELY angry, screaming out. Yelling so many things, he jumped down in the floor and sat with his feet and legs crossed and he looked like a stone Buddha statue, his facial expression was like a stone Buddha and he could not move. There was someone there on the prayer team that was getting aggravated at him because of his behavior (but in reality, the spirit that was speaking through him).

However, the demon started laughing and speaking to the person on the prayer team telling him, "You have sin, you have anger, you have sin, ha ha, ha ha ha!" It is so important that you and the people on your prayer team walk in love and obedience to God's Word. Treat the people with love and respect that you are ministering to, but to the devil we must speak in authority and in the name of Jesus command him (or them) to go.

This man had allowed the enemy access into his life, first of all, through false religions and trying to still play around with another religion of his ancestors. We cannot serve two masters. He also allowed to enemy to fill him with guilt and shame because years ago his girlfriend had an abortion and he took her to the location where they performed the abortion. He did not want her to have an abortion, he wanted the baby. He had been tormented for years about the abortion and that he was a part of it by taking her to have one even though it was against his wishes.

He also had a problem in the area of his thoughts concerning ministers, teachers and preachers of the Gospel. He said as he would sit and listen to them, he would have bad thoughts, judging, criticizing them, and mocking them in his thoughts as he would sit in the congregation and listen.

He really had many different spiritual issues he was dealing with, self-hatred, guilt, shame, pride, suicidal thoughts, and other issues. He allowed the thoughts to linger in his mind and opened the door for sadness, depression, addiction, suicidal thoughts, and the next step for him would have been death.

One door open to the enemy of guilt or shame and the enemy (unseen demonic forces) can come in and keep the door open for other spirits to come inside. Obviously, he allowed unclean thoughts in and meditated on the wrong things. This opened the door to an unclean spirit.

You will guard him and keep him in perfect and constant peace whose mind [both its inclination and its character] is stayed on You, because he commits himself to You, leans on You, and hopes confidently in You.

Isaiah 26:3 (AMP)

Walking in holiness before God is vital. It is not about works but obedience to the Word of God because we love Him.

The seriousness of what happens in the mind if we are not walking in holiness with God even in our thoughts is found in Isaiah Chapter 58. God sent a word of rebuke to the people, His people. Isaiah the prophet discovered the secret cause of the spiritual breakdown of God's people.

Cry aloud spare not lift up thy voice like a trumpet and show my people their transgressions and the house of Judah their sins.

Isaiah 58:1 (KJV)

God sent a piercing word of rebuke to a people who were seeking God.

Yet they seek me daily and delight to know my ways as a nation that did righteous and forsook not the ordinance of their God and they ask of me the ordinance of justice and delight in approaching to God.

Isaiah 58:2 (KJV)

A people that have set their heart on the Lord, anxious to get to church, sought the Lord daily, more than some in the churches may be doing daily these days. The people were attending church and outwardly they appeared to be hungry for God. Yet God said, "Show My people their sins." They delighted in hearing the Word. The Bible said they came to sit before Isaiah the Prophet; they loved to hear the Word but they didn't follow it. It only sounded like sweet words to them. They loved to hear it, but didn't act on it, they were not doers of the Word. They asked God for justice yet God said, "Show my people their transgressions and sins."

God sent a strong word of rebuke.

But your iniquities have separated between you and your God, and your sins have hidden His face from you, that He will not hear. What is the sin that He said, "Blow the trumpet loudly, pierce it, loudly?"

Isaiah 59:2 (KJV)

What kind of sin is it that He would pierce loudly, and give a very strong and loud warning? Their sin is hatching the cockatrice or snake eggs.

They hatch cockatrice' eggs, and weave the spider's web: he that eateth of their eggs dieth, and that which is crushed breaketh out into a viper.

Isaiah 59:5 (KJV)

The mind is the womb of the heart. Out of the abundance of the heart, the mouth speaks. There is a seed or a sperm that is placed there. And these are lying spirits that put evil thoughts in the mind, if those evil thoughts are not dealt with while they are just a seed, if they are not cast out, it is conceived, when lust is conceived it brings forth death. That is why we must cast it out immediately. It is a seed and will grow into an egg and inside the egg is a serpent and is poison and it will finally destroy you.

They went to church, but their minds had evil thoughts, ungodly thoughts, unloving thoughts, could be bitterness, resentment, jealousy, hatred, revenge, retaliation. The Bible says, "Enemy sows the seed /tares in the mind." God looks at what is going on inside the mind. Not just that you show up to church service and sing and outwardly praising the Lord. But God is looking at the thought life, "God said as a man thinks in his heart so is, he." God is not interested only in what you say, but what is in your heart. Their bodies were in the service but their hearts were not really there. They were fasting and praying, but they were not being heard.

Look at Isaiah 58:3, "Wherefore have we fasted, *say they*, and thou seest not? *Wherefore* have we afflicted our soul, and thou takest no knowledge? Behold, in the day of your fast ye find pleasure, and exact all your labors."

They were realizing we are seeking You daily and fasting. Why are we going through all this if it does not work? But it was their thought life. There is nothing harmless or innocent about evil thoughts. If they are not cast down immediately, they will poison your soul.

Behold, thou shalt call a nation that thou knowest not, and nations that knew not thee shall run unto thee because of the Lord thy God, and for the Holy One of Israel; for He hath glorified thee. Seek ye the Lord while He may be found, call ye upon Him while He is near: Let the wicked forsake his way, and the unrighteous man his thoughts: and let him return unto the Lord, and He will have mercy upon him; and to our God, for He will abundantly pardon. 'For my thoughts are not your thoughts, neither are your ways my ways,' saith the Lord. 'For as the heavens are higher than the earth, so are My ways higher than your ways, and My thoughts than your thoughts.'

Isaiah 55:5-9 (KJV)

For the weapons of our warfare are not carnal, but mighty through God to the pulling down of strong holds; Casting down imaginations, and every high thing that exalteth itself against the knowledge of God, and bringing into captivity every thought to the obedience of Christ.

II Corinthians 10:4 (KJV)

As soon as the devil puts that unloving or evil thought in your mind, you are to cast it down immediately. The Bible said Jesus's heel was to be placed on the head of the serpent and crush it. And the moment the thought comes, we must crush it with the heel of Jesus Christ, the name of Jesus. And believe it can be cast down and destroyed while it is only a seed before it is conceived. Casting down imaginations and everything that exalts itself against the knowledge of God, this is in the context of bringing down strong holds, the very verse before says bring down strongholds. If you let the thought linger, even seconds, if you flirt with it, play with it, it will take root in your mind, and become a stronghold in your life, your mind. These unloving and evil thoughts are like strong holds in your mind.

David Wilkerson in his sermon *Hatching Snake Eggs* list three different kinds of thoughts that are satanic nest eggs. Injurious thoughts, Fear mongering thoughts, and lustful thoughts.

I know from my own studies and experience in ministering deliverance over the years many of these satanic thoughts are caused by an unloving spirit.

There are injurious thoughts:
Words that were spoken about you and injured you and you say you can't overlook it; you just can't get over it. They are thoughts that you play over and over in your mind, you go to bed with them. Isaiah 59:5 says that, "if you crush the egg, a serpent breaks out."

If you have been injured, and so many are injured easily, easily offended, you can even go to church and be are robbed of the presence of God, robbed of the anointing, because we are playing and replaying something that was done to you in your mind. Maybe you feel like you are boiling inside, or you have a hard time getting rid of the thoughts, replay every word, it is a very, very dangerous place to be in.

If your husband or someone has wronged you or hurt you, pray for them and leave it in God's hand. Pray for them. The day will come they will answer to God.

Vengeance is God's "Vengeance is Mine" (Rom. 12:19, KJV).

False witnesses did rise up; they laid to my charge things that I knew not. They rewarded me evil for good to the spoiling of my soul. But as for me, when they were sick, my clothing was sackcloth: I humbled my soul with fasting; and my prayer returned into mine own bosom. I behaved myself as though he had been my friend or brother: I bowed down heavily, as one that mourneth for his mother. But in mine adversity, they rejoiced, and gathered themselves together: yea, the objects gathered themselves together against me, and I knew it not; they did tear me, and ceased not: With hypocritical mockers in feasts, they gnashed upon me with their teeth.

Psalm 35:11 – 16 (KJV)

Mine enemies speak evil of me, when shall he die, and his name perish? And if he come to see me, he speaketh vanity: his heart gathereth iniquity to itself; when he goeth abroad, he telleth it. All that hate Me whisper together against Me: against Me do they devise my hurt. An evil disease, say they, cleaveth fast unto him: and now that he lieth he shall rise up no more. Yea, mine own familiar friend, in whom I trusted, which did eat of my bread, hath lifted up his heel against me.

Psalm 41:5-9 (KJV)

If someone has hurt you or wounded you deeply, you must deal with it quickly. You may be carrying around something that has crushed your spirit, and you are replaying it or repeating it over and over again in your mind and you just can't seem to get over it. Maybe it was a close friend, a betrayal by your very own spouse, or someone you trusted, they ate at your table with you, hurt you. You cannot have victory in your life, you cannot grow in the Lord, you cannot maintain His presence until you kill that egg, don't hatch it anymore, or it will destroy you. Deal with it. Let the word of the Lord speak to you. You can't go on with it, and you must get free and there can be no freedom, until you repent for the unloving and unholy thoughts, forgive the person, release the one that hurt you. You need deliverance from it and God wants you delivered of it. You can't go on with these thoughts raging in your mind.

Jesus said, "I was the song of the drunkerd in the streets." Let them talk about you, let them rave, but don't let it destroy your spirit and your soul. The wicked speak lies and their poison is like the poison of snakes. They may even lie about you but God said, "Vengeance is Mine I will repay".

We see from the above scriptures that even though He was physically injured, He still loved them, even though He was lied about, and they tried to kill Him, He called them My friend. Jesus still loved those that hurt Him.

We are commanded to love one another as Christ loved us.

A new commandment I give unto you, that ye love one another; as I have loved you, that ye also love one another.

John 13:34 (KJV)

This is amazing love. While we were at enmity with God, He loved us. He died for us while we were still sinners. When we did not know God, when we did not love God, He died for us. This is how we are commanded to love everyone. Even our enemies, we must love them.

But God commendeth His love toward us, in that, while we were yet sinners, Christ died for us.

Romans 5:8 (KJV)

We must forgive those that have injured and wounded us. That means we need to get rid of unforgiveness, bitterness, resentment, revenge, et. These sins will open the door to the demonic in our lives if we are not obeying the commandment to forgive and to love.

Jesus Washed Judas Feet – His Betrayer

I know you probably have read in the Gospel of John Chapter thirteen about Jesus washing the disciple's feet. However, did you really understand that when He washed their feet he also washed Judas's feet, the one who was about to betray Him and Jesus knew that it was Judas who was going to betray Him and turn Him over to be tortured and crucified. Knowing all that and He still broke bread together, ate together, drank together, fed him, and even washed his feet.

Even after all the torture that Jesus endured, the whipping and beating that Jesus endured, the crown of thorns, the nails pounded into each of His hands and nails hammered into His feet and hanging on that cross and a sword that pierced His side. Innocent hanging on that cross, not a few drops but His blood poured out. He was raised from the dead, and when Jesus came up on the two disciples that did not recognize Jesus. They had their heads down discussing all the things that had happened with Jesus being crucified. They said, "Have you alone not heard all the things that have happened these days?" And Jesus replied, "What things?" Wow, that is so amazing! He is the one that went through all the betrayal and torture. He did not start to talk about how terrible a person Judas was. He did not talk about all the pain He suffered because of Judas. He already had let it go. He already forgave him. This is truly forgiveness when we can say, 'what things?' I'm not saying to forgive is easy to do, but if you want to live a victorious life lined up with the Word and pleasing to God, then you must forgive.

Fear Mongering Thoughts:

Thoughts that produce fear are very serious. God said 365 times in His Word, *FEAR NOT*. Many are hatching nest eggs of these serpents. Crippling Fear, "Fear has torment." These are fearful thoughts. There are so many kinds of fear. All fearful thoughts are fatal to your spiritual life if they are not dealt with immediately and is most dangerous of all.

If a woman is pregnant, the fear she has can also affect the baby in the womb. She may be afraid how will she take care of the child, not enough money, or the husband is abusive to her how will he be with the child, or she may be afraid of losing the child before he is born. This fear can transfer to the baby and cause the baby to be sick (I will not go into all that at this time but perhaps in another book).

People that are perfectionists think they can't please anybody. It is a driving fear. There are so many types of fear. Fear of losing your spouse. Fear of Disease. Fear of Failure.

We must deal with fear. You are in a spiritual warfare. God sees fear thoughts as so contagious, so dangerous that He must isolate it. When it is on someone, it is so poisonous it infects others. In Deuteronomy 20:8, "And the officers shall speak further unto the people, and they shall say, What man *is there that* is fearful and fainthearted? let him go and return unto his house, lest his brethren's heart faint as well as his heart."

He said the enemy is going to be stronger than any you have ever seen.

> *When thou goest out to battle against thine enemies, and seest horses, and chariots, and a people more than thou, be not afraid of them: for the Lord thy God is with thee, which brought thee up out of the land of Egypt. And it shall be, when ye are come nigh unto the battle, that the priest shall approach and speak unto the people, and shall say unto them, Hear, O Israel, ye approach this day unto battle against your enemies: let not your hearts faint, fear not, and do not tremble, neither be ye terrified because of them; For the Lord your God is he that goeth with you, to fight for you against your enemies, to save you.*
>
> Deuteronomy 20:1-4 (KJV)

God is saying I am your God. I have all power and authority. And I can save you. I am going to fight for you against your enemy to save you.

Maybe in your situation what you see ahead of you, it seems like these chariots are too big, it may seem overwhelming, there is no way out, humanly speaking, it may look hopeless. You may be thinking, *how am I going to do this?* God says, "If you are going to faint if you are going to be fearful go home and deal with it. If you are going to battle in the name of the Lord, there is only one thing that you are going to stand on. You are going to trust in My Word, and in My Power, and My authority and you are going to trust Me and that is it. You are going to believe what I have told you. That even though the enemy looks more powerful, even though it looks overwhelming, the odds are all against you, I am God, and I am with you!"

That is how you deal with fear. You must know and say, "I serve a God who has all power and all authority, God is with me! God is with me!" If you are repentant and walking in holiness God is with you! "If God be for us, who can be against us?" Whatever happens, I am in His hands and no man can pluck me out of it.

If you are fearful, a fainthearted person, with snake eggs hatching in your head, read Psalm chapter 27 verse five.

The Lord is my light and my salvation; whom shall I fear? The Lord is the strength of my life; of whom shall I be afraid? When the wicked, even mine enemies and my foes, came upon me to eat up my flesh, they stumbled and fell. Though an host should encamp against me, my heart shall not fear: though war should rise against me, in this will I be confident. One thing have I desired of the Lord, that will I seek after; that I may dwell in the house of the Lord all the days of my life, to behold the beauty of the Lord, and to inquire in his temple. For in the time of trouble he shall hide me in his pavilion: in the secret of his tabernacle shall he hide me; he shall set me up upon a rock.

Psalm 27:1-5 (KJV)

If we walk in His righteousness with clean hands and a pure heart, He is going to honor His promises to us. He says I have a secret place for you. When the enemy comes in like a roaring lion; He has a secret place for you. Even from the strife of tongues, I am going to hide you, He will hide us.

Those fearful thoughts are dangerous because you are accusing God of forgetting about you. It is dangerous because you are accusing Him of neglect. You are saying God does not care about me. He has forgotten all about me.

Thoughts of Lust:

You may not realize it, but lustful thoughts are dangerous. Every sensual and fornicating action, everything that our hands and our body do in the way of fornication always begins with a thought. Why is it someone can repent go back, repent go back to it? Someone can be delivered but go back to it? It is because an evil thought is planted by a lying spirit and it is not immediately cast down. If you give it thirty seconds, it is going to take root and become a stronghold. This is why God literally screams out at us in the scripture. Cast out that wicked thought! Cast down that wicked imagination! The moment it comes in deal with it! Call on the name of the Lord.

You have to look at it like this, a thought that came in my mind is not just a thought and a desire to go back and do something again. It is not just the desires of the flesh, that is not just my flesh talking, that is not innocent. That is the devil himself is speaking to me. That is the seed of Satan himself that will kill me, that will destroy me if I continue meditating and thinking negative thoughts for one more moment. Don't continue on this thought one more minute. Get on your face and before God. Cry out to God and repent, renounce the wrong thoughts, and say, "By the authority and in the name of Jesus, I break the power of the enemy that is trying to come against my mind, and my thoughts right now! God, you are the deliverer and I thank you for setting me free from the snare of the enemy. This is from the pits of hell. And deal with it for what it is. It is deadly, deadly, poison."

You've got to acknowledge right now that it is a lying spirit or a spirit that is not of God. If you continue with the thoughts, it is going to destroy you. Satan you are a liar, this is from hell. It will take you, take your family, it will take everything you have. No wonder the Bible says, resist the devil and he will flee from you. You have got to resist him at the very first thought that he throws at your mind.

There are consequences if a person does not cast down that wicked thought the moment it comes in.

Terrible consequences of not dealing with this matter of not killing these evil thoughts.

Four things will happen, and you can see it. Your feet will run to your evil deeds, you want crawl back you will run back.

Their feet run to evil, and they make haste to shed innocent blood. Their thoughts are thoughts of iniquity; desolation and destruction are in their paths and highways.

Isaiah 59:7 (KJV)

These are people that are backslidden, they have gone back to their sins. These are a people who were once free, but they turn back to their wickedness because they did not deal with it.

This is how all sin starts with a thought. Wrong thoughts are sinful. Everything you do that is wrong starts with a thought before you act on it. Before someone commits adultery, they thought about it and meditated on it before you act on it. Someone leaves with another man or another woman. Their feet are swift to evil. When the thoughts came, they flirted with it. Played with the thoughts. Now they are driven. The snake eggs have hatched and now they are running to their evil. Not even crying children can't stop him, spouse heartbroken can't stop them, nothing can stop them.

If you don't kill those thoughts, no one can stop you. Have you ever been around a Christian that used to be so gentle and kind and later you meet them and they are so cold, they don't even talk about Jesus. I can't believe how much they have changed. What is wrong with them? Their feet are running toward their evil now. They have allowed the viper eggs in their mind to hatch.

Their love of God has grown cold to the things of God. The affection of their first love is waxed cold and no longer desire to do the things that are pleasing to God. That is the first consequence when you won't kill it, there will be a driving spirit that will come. Satan has that snake hatched. That venom snake spirit will drive you to run to it, run to your sin. The venom will drive you to sin, you will run to the sin, and you will run toward the evil thoughts.

If someone has lustful thoughts and refuses to cast them down, meditated on it, and then goes out committing fornication or adultery, it is because a snake egg has hatched. You have played with it and toyed with it and finally you are out of control.

And the Bible says very clearly here in that same verse, "Their thoughts are thoughts of iniquity, wasting and destruction are in their paths." Nothing can stop them, they are just going to waste themselves from now on unless they take the thoughts captive, cast down the imagination and kill the snake egg.

A Loss of Peace

> *The way of peace they know not, and there is no justice or right in their goings. They have made them into crooked paths; whoever goes in them does not know peace.*
>
> Isaiah 59:8 (KJV)

Everyone that goes with them will lose their peace too. Someone goes into sin and you try to go with them you will lose your peace too. The most mixed up people in the world are those that once knew God but let their thoughts run wild. Have lost their peace completely and those that go with them will lose their peace too.

> *Therefore, are justice and right far from us, and righteousness and salvation do not overtake us. We expectantly wait for light, but [only] see darkness; for brightness, but we walk in obscurity and gloom. We grope for the wall like the blind, yes, we grope like those who have no eyes. We stumble at noonday as in the night; in dark places and among those who are full of life and vigor, we are as dead men.*
>
> Isaiah 59: 9-10 (KJV)

The peace is gone, nothing but darkness, and what has happened? The snake has hatched. Finally, they develop a Jekyll and Hyde personality. They become very changeable.

The Bear and Dove Syndrome-

We all groan and growl like bears and moan plaintively like doves. We look for justice, but there is none; for salvation, but it is far from us.

Isaiah 59:11 (KJV)

Someone that is a dove one minute and ready to chew you up the next. Temper! They roar like a bear then turn around and say, "I am so sorry, I am so sorry." They roar like bears and then become gentle like doves. This are spirits of anger and rage. There is no self-control. This is not the character and nature of God. It is the opposite of the fruit of the spirit, which is love kindness, gentleness, and self control. God does not want us to have this type of ungodly character! God will not have those wild tempers. The spirit of Christ is kind and gentle, and long suffering. And if you have got that bear and dove thing in you, then the spirit of God has to kill that snake in you, and it must be cast it out.

Maybe you know people like that? It is very serious. Why, it is in the mind. People think they can go to church and put on a front. Act holy while they are in church, but on the way to church there was screaming and yelling, disrespecting the spouse or family, maybe even someone in traffic on the way to church. This is happening around the world and God wants His people to walk in love and delivered from this bear syndrome.

An absolute promise that assures you that no evil thought need be conceived in your mind, an absolute promise is, "God will keep him in perfect peace whose mind is stayed on Him" (Isaiah 26:3, KJV). Keep your mind on Jesus, every time those thoughts come, think on Jesus. Whatsoever things are pure, honest, of a good report think on these things (Phil 4:8, KJV).

A person needs to recognize the bad temper, realize he is in sin, have had enough of living like that, and have a strong desire to be free from it, renounce it, say I will not have it in my life, I will no longer be a slave to this spirit and I really want to be delivered from it. I am not going to put up with it any longer. I am not going to be like that. Not only does this spirit cause the person to sin but also hurting other innocent people that are on the receiving end of your anger.

You should have the joy in your heart. Those that walk with God have that joy. Because there is that confidence in God. We should bear much fruit, love and joy are fruits of the spirit.

Therefore, gird up the loins of your mind. Be transformed by the renewing of your mind.

> *I will lift up mine eyes unto the hills, from whence cometh my help.*

My help cometh from the Lord, which made heaven and earth.

He will not suffer thy foot to be moved: he that keepeth thee will not slumber.

Behold, he that keepeth Israel shall neither slumber nor sleep.

The Lord is thy keeper: the Lord is thy shade upon thy right hand.

The sun shall not smite thee by day, nor the moon by night.

The Lord shall preserve thee from all evil: he shall preserve thy soul.

The Lord shall preserve thy going out and thy coming in from this time forth, and even for evermore.

Psalm 121 (KJV)

We must trust in the Lord and we must be ready to deal with those unholy thoughts. We must be ready to kill those snake eggs. Kill the thoughts by casting them out in the name of Jesus and destroy those snake eggs.

We must say, "I have had enough!" and get rid of the thoughts. Then God will come with a cleansing stream through our minds. Cleanse our thoughts. Cleanse our minds. Also, the washing of the water of the word will renew our mind and our thoughts.

If you have ANY un-forgiveness toward anyone, if you have a grudge, or if there has been a seed planted in your mind, a root of bitterness, fear, rebellion, lust; if you have been injured or wounded, God will deal with your heart and show you. Don't let it continue; it will poison you. Tell God, *I have had enough, I want to lay it down. Tell the Lord, I need to be delivered.* (Wilkerson, *Hatching Snake Eggs*, Sermon)

God's people must gain freedom from unholy thoughts and God will set people free if they desire, but make the step to submit to God, resist it and cast it out in the Name of Jesus.

CHAPTER SEVEN

Fear vs. Perfect Love

For God hath not given us the spirit of fear; but of power, and of love, and of a sound mind.

2 Timothy 8:15 (KJV)

The foundation to every disease and disorder is the breakdown of this commandment: Jesus spoke the words, "Thou shalt love the Lord thy God with all they heart, with all thy soul, and with all their mind. This is the first and greatest commandment. And the second is like unto it, thou shalt love they neighbor as thyself. On these two commandments, hang all the law and the prophets."

Dr. Henry Wright says this in his teachings on PTSD, "The foundation of the Bible, the foundation of all creation, the foundation of all sanity, the foundation of all health, the foundation for all mankind, for all of eternity is embraced in being reconciled to the Godhead:

the Father, the Word who is Jesus and the Holy Spirit. You being reconciled to yourself about yourself and being prepared to be reconciled to others."

The root of the issue is that many of us have been raised from generations who did not know how to care for each other and be a safe place. This is where fear has an open door. In the absence of love, fear comes in. It will develop a person not able to trust, to be easily overwhelmed and to feel unsafe and insecure. A separation occurs in relationships. This person begins to feel like they need to protect themselves from others. They may struggle connecting with others and with feelings of isolation and rejection. We are most vulnerable to the attacks of the enemy when we are isolated and disconnected.

"From this foundation of fear that the enemy has built into a person's life, he will use a traumatic event and the conversion of long-term memory to his advantage. Short-term memory is the processing of what we can see. Long-term memory occurs when we repeatedly return to or sustain a specific thought or thought pattern. A process called protein synthesis will develop this thought pattern into a permanent pathway using an element of RNA and DNA." (*Be in Health* Blog 06/2018)

What the enemy wants to do when a traumatic event occurs, is to cement that trauma into long term pathway in order to create the maximum possible bondage for a person. And he will intercept it.

I. Biological Manifestations Caused from Fear

The biological manifestations of this fear occur in a part of the brain called the amygdala. When this fear and projected fear becomes a long-term pathway of thought, one of the two sections of the amygdala becomes enlarged causing it to respond hyperactively. This in turn triggers the hypothalamus to respond in a state of fight or flight continually.

The hypothalamus is the gland responsible for secreting the chemicals for a fight or flight reaction in the body in response to a dangerous situation. If it is releasing these stress chemicals continually, it only takes a small trigger of thought or outside stimulus to trigger the secretion of excessive chemicals that will produce the feeling of panic and phobic realities. This is the physiological phenomenon of PTSD.

The enemy can control the body with this one gland, if he can control our spirituality and our soul - our thought processing. If we don't understand our own minds, we are nothing more than a puppet on a string.

Fear will have us meditate on the failures of our past and project them into the future. The enemy does not want us to receive that forgiveness that the Father has freely offered us, or to be able to forgive others.

We are not called to be victims and we must be freed from the effects of fear or PTSD. The place of safety is in the Father God. It is important to seek His heart and learn who He really is through His Word; His love, His Grace and His mercy. God will help them process and overcome the traumatic event. It will still be a memory from the past, but then they have received healing in their heart, they will not have all the feelings of hurt and fear attached to it.

The person must cast down the fear and make fear the enemy. "For we wrestle not against flesh and blood, but against principalities, against powers, against rulers of the darkness of this world, against spiritual wickedness in high places." (Ephesians 6:12, KJV)

There is a "spirit of fear." Fear needs to be dealt with; it needs to be recognized, repented for and cast out in the name of Jesus. The person can, "then lay hands on the one who is afflicted and command the amygdala to come back down to its proper size by the power of the Holy Spirit." Then establish the Word in his heart as a firm foundation. Do not allow the fear to come back in with doubt and unbelief and become unstable in all his ways. Otherwise, we are not able to recover ourselves out of the snare of the enemy.

We choose to believe the thoughts that fear has projected into our lives or believe the Word of God. We must, "cast down imaginations, and every high thing that exalts itself against the knowledge of God and bring into captivity every thought to the obedience of Christ" (2 Corinthians 10:5, KJV).

The Holy Spirit will lead us and guide us through and be fully restored to the fullness of life that He has prepared for us.

II. Fear Affects the Mind

A mother asked us to pray for her thirteen-year-old daughter. One day, while the mother and father were at home, their daughter that had been outside ran inside the house upset and into the kitchen and grabbed a knife and was running outside ready to stab one of the other teenagers in the neighborhood. Her father grabbed her to stop her from going outside with the knife. Her whole demeanor had changed into rage and her eyes looked as if someone else was looking out of them at her father and mother as they held on to her. The mother started speaking in the name of Jesus to stop the girl. The father asked his wife if she saw the look in the girl's eyes before she started speaking, "Stop in the name of Jesus!" They both saw it.

This teenager had been bullied and mistreated by someone in her past that she believed she could trust.

She was asked to come outside in her neighborhood and hangout for a while and she gladly said yes and went to meet them however, once she went where they asked to meet her, the person she believed to be friend started beating her up and the other person was recording it on his phone camera to post it on the internet. The girl was so hurt by what happened. How could they do such a thing? she thought and why would they would do such a thing to her? She had never done anything to wrong them before. After this horrific incident, although she suffered going through the physical fight she was in much more mental pain and distress afterward. The betrayal was almost more than she could deal with. This precious young girl decided to learn how to defend herself. She started going to the internet and watching videos of people fighting so she could learn how to fight. Then watching video teachings on how to fight and hurt people.

She allowed anger to build up inside of her toward others, then opened the door in her life to rage, and was willing to bully others to try to scare others from trying to mess with her. All this started with the fear of the moment she was betrayed and became so frightened after this traumatic event in her life. At that young tender age, she allowed her heart to become hardened.

You see, God clearly warns us in His Word that we can be angry but not to the point of sin. "Be angry, and sin not." Also, "Do not let the sun go down on your wrath and give no place to the devil." If we continue in the anger we can give place to the devil in our lives and it will give legal authority to the enemy to oppress us.

Spiritual warfare is primarily a matter of the mind. As long as the mind is held in check and is renewed to right thinking by the Word of God, the majority of spiritual attacks will fail. However, when the mind is left open and unguarded, it becomes the primary battlefield Satan uses to destroy lives, finances, businesses, marriages, emotions, and so on.

This is why one of your most important responsibilities is to stand guard over your mind. In doing so, you are actually placing a guard around every other battlefield in your life!

Exercise foresight and be on the watch to look [after one another], to see that no one falls back from and fails to secure God's grace (His unmerited favor and spiritual blessing), in order that no root of resentment (rancor, bitterness, or hatred) shoots forth and causes trouble and bitter torment, and the many become contaminated and defiled by it.
Hebrews 12:15 (KJV)

Keep and guard your heart with all vigilance and above all that you guard, for out of it flow the springs of life.
Proverbs 4:23 (KJV)

Put on the whole armor of God that you may be able to stand against the wiles of the devil.

Ephesians 6:11 (KJV)

The word "against" in the Greek denotes a forward position or a face-to-face encounter. A soldier so bold and daring, and courageous that he is glaring fearlessly right into the eyes of his adversary. (Renner, *Dressed to Kill*, 87)

This clearly demonstrates that, with God's mighty power and His armor on our side, we are more than a match for the enemy. In fact, we are a threat to Satan's domain! Never be in fear at the thought of what the devil may do.

The word *wiles* (in the Greek is *methodos*) means 'with a road.' "If the devil operates on one single avenue, what is the destination that diabolical road is headed toward?" The mind.

Another important word to understand when discussing spiritual warfare is the word *devices*. In 2 Cor 2:11, Paul gives us a clue as to where this road leads that the devil is traveling on. Paul says, "We are not ignorant of his [Satan's] devices." (Devices in the Greek is *noemata* and the meaning is the mind). The form Paul used here carries the idea of a deceived mind. Specifically, this word noemata denotes the insidious and malevolent plot of Satan to fill the human mind with confusion. (Renner *Dressed to Kill*, 92) This means that he is operating in a seemingly harmless way, but actually with grave effect. He is wishing and planning evil or harm to others.

Devices bears the notion of mind games. You could translate the verse "We are not ignorant of the mind games that Satan tries to pull on us."

It was for this reason that Paul said, "Casting down imaginations, and every high thing that exalted itself against the knowledge of God, and bringing into captivity *every thought* to the obedience of Christ" (2 Corinthians 10:5, KJV).

The devil loves to make a playground out of people's minds! He delights in filling their emotions and senses with illusions that captivate their minds and ultimately destroy them.

We must make a mental decision to take charge of our minds, "Bringing into captivity every thought to the obedience of Christ." Stop listening to ourselves and start speaking to ourselves!

Where is the road headed? The word "devices" clearly demonstrates that this road of the devil is headed toward the mind. If the devil can control a person's mind, he can also control that person's health and emotions. He seeks to penetrate a person's mental control center, so he can flood it with deception and falsehood. Once this is accomplished, the devil can then begin to manipulate that person's body and emotions from a position of control.

When Satan succeeds in penetrating and paving a road into a person's mind and emotions, the process of mental and spiritual captivity in that person's life is well under way. What comes next is up to the individual who is under attack. He can abort this devilish process by renewing his mind with the Word and by allowing God's power to do a work within him. But if that person does not choose to renew his mind and yield to the work of the Holy Spirit, it will be only a matter of time before a solid stronghold of deception begins to dominate and manipulate his self-image, his emotional status, and his overall thinking (Renner, *Dressed to Kill*, 200)

III. The Deception of the Devil

Deception occurs when a person believes the lies that the enemy has been telling him. The moment someone begins to accept Satan's lies as truth, is the very moment those wicked thoughts and mind games begin to produce the devil's reality in his life.

For instance, the devil may assault your mind by repeatedly telling you that you are a failure or something you did in your past was so horrendous that can't seem to get over it. However, as long as you resist those demonic allegations, they will exert absolutely no power in your life.

But what if you begin to give credence to these lies and to mentally perceive them as the actual truth? Those lies will then begin to control you and to dominate your emotions and your thinking. In the end, your faith in those lies will give power to them and will cause them to create a bona fide reality in your life - *and you will become a failure or even have self-hatred.* This is a manifestation of completed deception.

Sadly, as Christians continue to pay attention to those lying insinuations, the door remains open for the devil to continue pounding away at that person's mind and preying on his emotions. After a period of time, the person's mind battered and weary from worrying - begins to believe those false allegations. The faith in the lying emotions may then empower the lies to become a reality in his life.

By mentally embracing these false insinuations, the person opens the door for the enemy to penetrate his mind. Thus, the process of confusion is implemented; mind games are set in motion; and that believer's perception of things becomes twisted and bent. If this seducing, deceiving process is not stopped at this point, it is probably only a matter of time before the weary minded believer begins to embrace these mental lies as though they were really the truth.

What is the end result of the devil's deception? When believers falsely believe that their marriage is on the rocks, that they will die of a terminal disease, or that they have no hope for the future, they open the door for the enemy to move these lying suggestions from the thought realm into the natural realm where they become a bona fide reality. These believer's false perceptions empower the lies, and the devil uses those false beliefs to create HIS reality in the natural realm!

Perhaps the enemy has constantly bombarded your mind about sickness that runs in your family medical history. Family members have died from the disease. Perhaps his lying allegations have repeatedly told you that you are going to contract a terrible disease and die an early death. When these lies first assaulted your mind, you resisted them and refused to believe what you were hearing. Now, however, you have begun to wonder if these thoughts may have some validity.

If you don't stop this process, it will only be a matter of time until you truly begin to feel physically sick in your body. Do not give credence to those lying insinuations! When you embrace the devil's mind games and perceive them as truth, you give power to them!

If you do not take charge of your mind and begin to speak God's truth to yourself to combat the devil's lies, the complete process of deception will continue working in your life. Eventually the process will be complete, and your fears will become reality. When this occurs, you will be deceived in that area of your life.

It is extremely important to understand what God's Word says about the wiles of the devil, especially when studying the subject of spiritual warfare. We must use the authority that has been given to us and know that we have this authority over all the power of the enemy just as God tells us in Luke 10:19. He has also given us His name. So, in the name of Jesus, command those fearful thoughts, ungodly thoughts to go. Command the enemy to go from you in the name of Jesus the Christ of Nazareth.

In spiritual warfare it is vital and necessary that we must maintain a life filled with love, even our thoughts filled with love. This will protect us from the devices of the enemy. This perfect love will cast out thoughts and suggestions made by the enemy. Love will cast out fear. It is vital that we put in practice and exercise this love in our lives daily to thwart the plans of the enemy against our minds. "And herein do I exorcise myself, to have always a conscience void of offense toward God, and toward men" (Acts 24:16, KJV). It takes an effort, and Paul compares it to exercising.

The Bible teaches us that one of the ways we can keep from being drawn back into unforgiveness or the thoughts of being wronged, injured or hurt is to pray for the person. "But I say to you, love your enemies, bless those who curse you, do good to those who hate you, and pray for those who spitefully use you and persecute you" (Matthew 5:44, KJV).

If we do not guard our hearts from fear of what others are saying or doing against us, we can become filled with sorrow. "Fierce witnesses rise up; they ask me things I do not know. They reward me evil for good, to the sorrow of my soul" (Psalms 35:11-12, KJV). We see in the next verses how David overcame those who tried to lie about him and destroy him. He said, "But as for me, when they were sick, my clothing was sackcloth; I humbled myself with fasting; and my prayer would return to my own heart. I paced about as though he were my friend or brother; I bowed down heavily, as one who mourns for his mother" (Psalms 35:13-14, KJV).

David's response was not based on the actions of others. He determined to do what was right, he prayed for them as if they were his close brothers or as one grieving the loss of a mother. We should pray the very things for them that we want God to do for us. As we pray for the person that has wronged us and do good to them, our hearts are being exorcised to stay free from offense and fear. We are exorcising our hearts to love, and we will grow spiritually and develop a mature love (Bevere Bait of Satan, 148).

"And above all things have fervent love for one another, for love will cover a multitude of sins" (1 Peter 4:8, KJV). And this is pleasing to God. One-way love will cover the sin is that the person that has been wronged will forgive and not replay the sin over and over again. The person forgives, and therefore, he is not in sin by holding unforgiveness in his own heart.

CHAPTER EIGHT

Demonic Intimidation

There was a healthy lady that had been in fear for many years that she would get the same disease that her grandfather and her mother had. Cancer ran in her family and though she was healthy the enemy (the devil) had put the thoughts in her mind for years that she was going to get cancer. At the age forty-seven, while during one of her checkups at the doctors office, she received her test results back that they saw something that was cancerous in her cervical area and the doctors recommended a simple procedure to have them removed. She and her husband agreed and scheduled to have them removed. During the procedure while the doctor was removing one of the cancerous tumors, it shattered into many tiny pieces and became too small to remove.

She was then seen by another specialist about this and doctors recommended that she receive the strongest chemotherapy known to man to get rid of it before it spreads throughout her body. As these specialists described what she would have to endure during and after, as well as the side effects of this type of chemo, such as temporary insanity, she cried heavily thinking this is worse than she ever imagined before.

All those years that she was healthy, she allowed the devil to steal her peace. She listened to him constantly whisper threats about her future. We met with her and her husband and prayed. We led her to renounce the fear that she allowed to come into her life. Then by the power of God and in the name of Jesus broke every generational curse off of her life and commanded by the authority and in the name of Jesus for the sickness to come out by the roots and to leave her body.

They received the ministry, she and her husband loved God and their faith was increasing and began confessing words of faith and that Jesus had healed her. She would not listen any longer to those whispers in her mind about what was going to happen to her. Although they had faith and hope, with some hesitation they decided to go forward with the doctor's instructions to go through what the doctors recommended with the chemo. They actually left to go out of state to Texas with plans to live there for three months and receive the chemo. All the way there and after arrival they confessed God's Word that Jesus is the Healer and by

His stripes she was healed. She had to take more MRI tests and scans before starting the Atomic Chemo. The doctors needed to meet with them again and discus the current test results. They were in awe at the test results! The doctors gave them a piece of paper with the initials NEOD, No Evidence of Disease! The Scan showed nothing at all, not even a trace of cancer! The doctors said she did not need the chemo! ALL the glory to God and our Lord and Savior Jesus Christ!

The devil has been lying and deceiving mankind since the first man Adam and we see his cunningness and trickery throughout the Bible. We see in First Samuel 17, how the devil used Goliath's lying allegations to intimidate and confuse the armies of Israel. Goliath's arrogant, boastful and proud declarations of the Israelite's demise was so effective that not one soldier from the Hebrew camp was willing to stand up to this aggressor. The Israelite army was rendered functionally paralyzed for forty days - until a courageous young man named David came along with the power of God to challenge those lies!

And the Philistines stood on a mountain on the one side, and Israel stood on a mountain on the other side: and there was a valley between them. And there went out a champion out of the camp of the Philistines, named Goliath, of Gath, whose height was six cubits and a span.

1 Samuel 17: 3-4 (KJV)

No wonder the Israelites were intimidated by Goliath! The appearance alone of this giant would be intellectually and emotionally overwhelming. Goliath was 9 feet 9 inches, almost 10 feet tall!

And he had a helmet of brass upon his head, and he was armed with a coat of mail; and the weight of the coat was five thousand shekels of brass. And he had greaves of brass upon his legs, and a target of brass between his shoulders. And the staff of his spear was like a weaver's beam; and his spear's head weighed six hundred shekels of iron: and one bearing a shield went before him.

1 Samuel 17: 5-7 (KJV)

Goliath was armed to the max! And if Goliath wore that much weaponry, imagine how much the giant must have weighed himself!

Yet it wasn't Goliath's size or his weaponry the caused the Israelites to shrink back in fear. What did cause the Israelites to fear? The constant threats and mental bombardment that Goliath hit them with every single day. This mental harassment crippled the Hebrew soldiers so that they lost sight of the awesome ability of God.

Concerning these continued threats of Goliath, the Bible says:

And he stood and cried unto the armies of Israel, and said unto them, "Why are ye come out to set your battle in array? Am not I a Philistine, and ye servants to Saul? Choose you a man for you and let him come down to me. If he be able to fight with me, and to kill me, then will we be your servants: but if I prevail against him, and kill him, then shall ye be our servants, and serve us." And the Philistine said, "I defy the armies of Israel this day; give me a man, that we may fight together.

1 Samuel 17: 8-10 (KJV)

These threats of the huge, Goliath were so emotionally overpowering the next verse declares, "When Saul and all Israel heard those words of the Philistine, they were dismayed, and greatly afraid" (1 Samuel 17: 11, KJV).

Goliath mentally and emotionally immobilized the armies of Israel without ever using a sword or spear! With words alone, he incapacitated, disabled, stunned, numbed, and disarmed the Israelites. The giant's flagrant and preposterous distortion of his own greatness was so outrageous that his words bewitched the listening Israelite army until they were controlled by his words

The devil is a slanderer and an accuser! Today, the devil still seeks to instill fear in believers the same way he paralyzed the Israelite army with fear through Goliath. The devil puts some people in fear and under his control. Still today this mental tool of the devil is used to assault the minds of believers. He bombards them with threatening thoughts such as you've been wronged or wounded, if you allow them to treat you like this you will look weak, you must get revenge, you have to return insult for insult, return evil for evil. This is the enemy's attempts to beat a hole through your mind and emotions, so you cannot think rationally he comes to pave a road of doubt and fear into your mind and fill your mind full of fear and confusion that you eventually lose the courage you need to step out in faith and obey God's Word to love.

If you meditate on the wrong thoughts, and on the Devil's threats long enough, you will become dismayed and greatly afraid, just like the children of Israel who listened to the words of Goliath and became functionally paralyzed by fear for forty days. You'll find yourself living on the low side of the victory unwilling to take on new challenges for fear that you might not be loved back, fear of being wounded or hurt again, for fear of what others might say, etc.

The devil wants to take you captive and destroy you with the same tools Goliath used against the Israelites. Satan wants to ruin your effectiveness and your walk with God.

In the midst of all of Goliath lies, the giant didn't make one statement that was true in verse nine. He said in effect, "If one of your number is able to fight me and win, we will serve you for the rest of our lives. But if I win, YOU Will serve us!"

These are hard facts for battle and are still the rules of spiritual warfare today.

If you conquer all the lying emotions, deceptive suggestions that the devil tries to use you will be able to keep the enemy in a subordinate position for the rest of your life once you stop Satan's intimidating threats and lies, he will no longer be able to hold your mind captive. You will be able to love freely.

If, however you do not learn how to take your thoughts captive your mind and your emotions will be used as tools of Satan to dominate your thought processes for the rest of your life. If you do not take charge of your mind, learning how to seek God's truth for yourself rather than listen to the enemies lies, the devil will continue to use lying emotions and illusions to manipulate, dominate, and control you for the rest of your life.

Noticed that Goliath said "...I defy the armies of Israel this day ...". (1 Samuel 17:10, KJV). Today the devil is still breathing out the same kind of terrorizing statements against the people of God, such as:

"I defied you to believe that your financial situation is going to turnaround."

"I defy you to believe your will ever have a good marriage."

"I defy you to believe you will prosper."

"I defy you to believe that your husband or wife will ever change."

"I defy you to believe you can love that one that wounded you."

Although the wicked Philistines never lifted a sword, threw a sphere, or budged from their encampment, they conquered the people of God with mental and verbal attacks of intimidation. The Israelites wrongly considered and meditated on Goliath's threats, allowing those threats to flood them with fear. As a result, they were neutralized without a ground war ever taken place!

Goliath made those threats often. The Word says, "And the Philistine drew near morning and evening and presented himself forty days" (I Samuel 17:16, KJV) Day and night, morning and evening, Goliath came to mentally undo the people of God.

This is how the enemy still attacks people's minds and emotions. He doesn't strike once and then come back a week later to strike again. Morning and evening the devil attacks, intent on his goal of irreparably damaging people's faith and confidence. Trying to kill and destroy their ability to maintain a life of love.

First Samuel 17:12,14,15,20,23:

Now David was the son of that Ephrathite of Bethlehemjudah, his name was Jesse; and he had eight sons… and David was the youngest: and the three eldest followed Saul. But David went and returned from Saul to feed his father's sheep at Bethlehem…And David rose early in the morning,… Sheep with the keeper, in took, and went, as Jesse had commended him [take food to his brothers], behold, there came up the champion, the Philistine of Gath, Goliath by name, out of the armies of the Philistines, and spake according to the same words: and David heard them.

Notice that verse 23 says, "…And David heard them." This was David's first encounter with the foreboding giant, and something in Goliath's words incited anger in David's soul. What a shock it was for this young shepherd to hear a pagan Philistine insulting the God of Israel and to realize that no one was doing anything about it! In fact, the Israelites weren't just sitting around doing nothing about Goliath. Verse 24 says they actually ran in terror: "And all the men of Israel, when they saw the man fled from him, and were sore afraid."

But David wasn't afraid of this Philistine giant - he was annoyed by Goliath's verbal arrogance!

And David spake to the man that stood by him saying, "What shall be done to that man that kills the Philistine, and take away the reproach from Israel? For whom is this uncir-

cumcised Philistine, that he should defy the armies of the living God"

I Samuel 17:26 (KJV)

There is a true boldness that the Holy Spirit gives to surrendered vessels. David was that yielded vessel. He was so surrendered to God's power working through him that a Holy Spirit inspired confidence rose up within him. At that point, David could not hold back his righteous anger! David was stunned by the fear that possessed the huge Israelite soldiers. He asked them, "Isn't there a cause here worth fighting for? Why aren't we fighting?"

Naturally speaking, David was no match for Goliath! However, David had heaven's perspective he knew that the outward man– the flesh–counted for nothing when it came to moving in the supernatural power of God! So David responded to Saul's doubts with words of faith, "...Your servant kept his father's sheep, and there came a lion, and a bear, and took a lamb out of the flock and I went out after him."

Goliath wasn't the first enemy David had faced in life–he already had confrontations with both the lion and a bear! As a shepherd, David had determined that those devourers would not steal one thing from him. That was the attitude David needed to defeat his enemy every time he struck.

We must have the same attitude; we must boldly declare to the enemy, "You cannot, cannot, cannot." If the devil doesn't willingly release that what is ours like David responded when the lion and the bear attacked his sheep. David told Saul, "And I went out after him, smote him and delivered it out of his mouth: and when he rose against me I caught them by beard and smote him, slew both the lion and the bear."

In the same way, we have to "go out after" the devil in the authority of Jesus name that he has given us enforcing to release whatever he has seized from us against our wills! David could now look straight into the face of this conflict with Goliath.

Thy servant slew both the lion and the bear: and this uncircumcised Philistine Shall be as one of them, seeing he hath defied the armies of the living God.

I Samuel 17:36, 39 (KJV)

David was empowered by the power of God. Goliath could not see the spiritual weapons.

And the Philistine came near unto David; and the man that carry the shield went before him. And when the Philistine looked about, and Saw David, he disdained him: for he was but a youth, and ruddy, and of a fair countenance. And the

Philistine said unto David, am I a dog that you come to me with staves? And the Philistine cursed David by his gods.

I Samuel 17:41-43 (KJV)

Goliath began to use his tools of mental and verbal harassment, just like the devil does today. Attempting to intimidate David and paralyze him with fear "...the Philistine said to David, 'Come to me, and I will give you your flesh to the fowls of the air, and to the beast of the field.'" Just as the entire army of Israel had been functionally immobilized for forty days by Goliath's outrageous claims, now the Philistine giant was proceeding to use the same strategy again in attempt to immobilize and paralyze David.

If David had turned his eyes from the Lord and stop meditating on His faithfulness, he would have begun to consider what Goliath had to say. Soon, those threats would have immobilized David, just as they have immobilized the armies of Israel.

But before the Giants threats had an opportunity to take root in his soul and produce paralyzing fear, David spoke forth his declaration of war against the enemy:

Then said David to the Philistine, 'Thou comest to me with a sword, and with a spear, and with a shield: but I come to thee in the name of the Lord of hosts, the God of the armies of Israel, whom thou hast defied. This day will the Lord deliver thee into mine hand; and I will smite thee, and take thine head from thee; and I will give the carcases of the host of the Philistines this day unto the fowls of the air, and to the wild beasts of the earth; that all the earth may know that there is a God in Israel. And all this assembly shall know that the Lord saveth not with sword and spear: for the battle is the Lord's, and He will give you into our hands.

I Samuel 17:45-47 (KJV)

Once David made his declaration of war, he wasted no time. Verse 48 says, "And it came to pass, when the Philistine arose, and came and drew near to meet David, that David hasted."

This must have shocked Goliath! Most challengers ran away from him, but David "Hastened." In other words, when the moment of conflict finally came and David saw Goliath coming, he picked up his sling and his five stones and ran toward the giant.

And David put his hand in his bag, inserted a stone and slang it, and smote the Philistine in his forehead, that stone sunk into his forehead; and he fell upon his face to the earth. So, David prevailed over the Philistine with a sling and with the stone, and smote the Philistine, and slew him.

I Samuel 17: 49-50 (KJV)

David wanted to make sure the job was finished!

But there was no sword in the hand David. Therefore, David ran, and stood upon the Philistine, and took his sword, and drew it out of the sheath thereof, and slew him, and cut off his head therewith. And when the Philistines saw their champion was dead, they fled.

I Samuel 17:50,51 (KJV)

Many people are mentally harassed and emotionally tormented by the adversary. Natural weapons will not help us in our fight with unseen, spiritual enemies.

We must cast down imaginations, and every high thing that exalteth itself against the knowledge of God and bringing into captivity every thought to the obedience of Christ.

Because of God's great love toward us, He has given us authority and power over the enemy to use His name, to command the enemy to flee, command negative thoughts to be cast down in the mighty name of Jesus the Christ of Nazareth.

CHAPTER NINE

Jesus the Deliverer

God tells us in His Word that many people are healed as they are delivered from demonic oppression. This aspect of the ministry of Jesus, healing, and deliverance, was interwoven. Many times, deliverance was needed to receive healing. It was so important that Jesus went from town to town casting out evil spirits and healing those that were oppressed by the devil. The great commission that Jesus told all of us to do is what He did and even more. It is vitally important to know God's Word concerning healing and deliverance for our own lives and how to minister and help others to be set free from sickness and disease caused by demonic oppression. We must also understand the importance of sanctification in maintaining our deliverance.

I. Jesus Healed the Sick and Cast Out Devils

The greatest way to know how we are to live our lives, is first of all through Jesus and His Word. It is very clear in the ministry of Jesus, that God does want His people to live healed, whole, and free from sicknesses and diseases as well as those caused by demonic oppression. "God anointed Jesus of Nazareth with the Holy Spirit and with power, who went about doing good and in particular healing all that were oppressed of the devil, for God was with him (Acts 10:38, AMP). All were healed by Jesus. "That means everyone who was healed under the ministry of Jesus was oppressed of the devil. In other words, the devil had something to do with their sickness. That doesn't mean an evil spirit was always present. It just means the devil was behind the whole situation. They were oppressed of the devil – every one of them" (Hagin, *Believer's Authority*, 2). "The greatest hinderance to healing is not believing that it is God's will to heal us. In order to benefit from or receive healing, the recipient must believe that the healing power is present." "Jesus is the will of God in Action" (Hagin, *Believer's Authority*, 57)

Jesus was Anointed to Heal the Brokenhearted

God is also concerned about our emotions and our hearts; that they are healed as well. Many suffer from different types of abuses, emotional abuse, verbal abuse, physical abuse by others in past or current relationships. Many are victims and they are left with emotional scars.

The Spirit of the Lord is upon Me, because He hath anointed me to preach the Gospel to the poor; He hath sent me to heal the brokenhearted, to preach deliverance to the captives, and recovering of sight to the blind, to set at liberty them that are bruised.

Luke 4:18 (KJV)

We must remember and remind others that we are not to have the victim mentality. Jesus will heal their broken hearts and set them free. We are not to have a victim mentality because we are victors, we have the victory because of Jesus, we have our liberty, and we are free in Christ. We must allow Him to be Lord over every area of our lives and not continually allow the past to project into the present or future.

Spirits of Infirmity Cast Out

Scriptures tell us there was a woman who had a spirit of infirmity for eighteen years and it had bowed her together that she could not lift herself up. After Jesus laid His hands on her, the demonic spirit left her then she was healed and able to lift herself. She was a daughter of Abraham, which means she was a believer in God. It is clear here that children of God can be oppressed of demonic spirits that cause sickness.

Unclean Spirits Cast Out

There are also many other scriptures that tell us that Jesus cast out evil spirits out of people while they were actually in the synagogue, which shows they were there to worship yet had spiritual issues or demonic oppression. The man in the synagogue with an unclean spirit, Jesus cast it out with a word and the demons left him. We must learn what will allow demonic spirits access into our lives and how to be free from them.

Deaf and Dumb Spirits Cast Out

God also teaches us in Ephesians Chapter 6, that there are different levels of demonic spirits. "For we wrestle not against flesh and blood but against principalities, against powers, against rulers of the darkness of this world, against spiritual wickedness in high places."

This is evident in the story of the man with the epileptic son in Mark 9:17. He had seizures and the demon would often throw him in the water or fire and harm him. Jesus delivered the son from the deaf and dumb spirit. He told the disciples that this kind only comes out by prayer and fasting referring to different levels of demons or demonic powers. Today, some wonder why the more powerful demons are not cast out, but the answer lies in the fact that the Church needs to rediscover this key to deliverance – the ministry of prayer and fasting.

Jesus also spoke to the father about the importance of faith to believe. *Now the father made an appeal to Jesus which is reminiscent of so many who came for healing. He said, "But if You can do anything, have compassion on us, and help us"* (Mark 9:22, KJV). Such as statement is not of faith, and Jesus could not let it pass. There must be no casting off of responsibility to put the failure on others. All must contribute their share in believing or accept their share of the failure. Jesus rebuked him gently by saying, "If you can believe, all things are possible to him who believes."

Regardless of how the afflicted child showed His compassion, Jesus would keep before his eyes the fact that healing is not based on need, but on faith. "But if you can do anything, have compassion on us, and help us" is the kind of statement that is just the opposite of faith. Jesus had to correct it. The poor father in his distress broke down and cried and said in faltering words, "Lord, I believe; help my unbelief." It was a pathetic request, but one that was irresistible. Jesus then turned to the boy:

When Jesus saw that the people came running together, He rebuked the unclean spirit, saying to it, "Deaf and dumb spirit, I command you, come out of him and enter him no more!" Then the spirit cried out, convulsed him greatly, and came out of him. And he became as one dead, so that many said, 'He is dead.'"

Mark 9:25,26 (KJV)

II. Sanctification

"Seventy to eighty percent of all disease in America with the name syndrome or incurable attached to it, has a spiritual root. ... defects that come because of separation from God and His Word, or deal with sanctification and sin and the resultant diseases" (Wright *More Excellent Way*, 27)

Who [the Lord} forgiveth all thine iniquities; who healeth all thy diseases?

Psalm 103:3 (KJV)

Fools because of their transgression, and because of their iniquities, are afflicted. Their soul abhorreth all manner of meat; and they draw near unto the gates of death. Then they cry unto the Lord in their trouble, and He saveth them out of their distresses. He sent His word, and healed them, and delivered them from their destructions.

Psalm 107:17-20 (KJV)

The children of Israel took themselves out from under the protection of their covenant by wrongdoing.

We have a New Covenant better than the Old Covenant. Yes, we have divine protection, but it is possible to take ourselves out from under the protection of this covenant. Sometimes as a result of not obeying God in some areas as we should. (Hagin, *Following God's Plan*, 5)

Jesus had just healed someone, and He made this statement, "Go your way and sin no more, lest a worse thing come upon you."

Afterward Jesus findeth him in the temple, and said unto him, Behold, thou art made whole: sin no more, lest a worse thing come unto thee.

John 5:14 (KJV)

The Lord Himself, our Savior, Healer, and Deliverer directly tied the lack of sanctification to disease. Jesus said, "Lest a worse thing come upon thee." Also, Scripture tells us that when a demon goes out of a person that it tries to come back again and brings seven more demons, and the condition of that person can be worse.

And the very God of peace sanctify you wholly: and I pray God your whole spirit and soul and body be preserved blameless unto the coming of our Lord Jesus Christ.

I Thessalonians 5:23 (KJV)

Is any sick among you? Let him call for the elders of the church; and let them pray over him, anointing him with oil in the name of the Lord: And the prayer of faith shall save the sick, and the Lord shall raise him up; and if he has committed sins, they shall be forgiven him.

James 5:14-15 (KJV)

In these verses, we see the lack of sanctification in a believer's life and the consequence, which shows us the relationship of sin to disease. People have gone into captivity because they have no knowledge. They had no discernment. In Hosea 4:6, God said, "My people perish for lack of knowledge." They had no discernment. And Hebrews 5:14 tells us that strong meat belongs to those that are full aged, even those that by reason of use have their senses exercised to discern both good and evil. Not just good- you must be able to discern evil also. One must recognize that they have a problem, repent, renounce it (turn away from it). We must submit ourselves to God and resist the devil and he will flee. God's people must recognize issues (sin) in their lives such as anger, bitterness, sadness, hopelessness, resentment, pride, unforgiveness; anything that God's Word warns us not to have. Once we repent, it is forgiven as if it never happened, washed in the blood of Jesus. We must renounce which means we will turn from doing those sinful acts of disobedience against God and His Word.

"Brethren, if a man be overtaken in a fault, ye which are spiritual, restore such a one in the spirit of meekness; considering thyself, lest thou also be tempted. Bear ye one another's burdens, and so fulfill the law of Christ. For if a man think himself to be something, when he is nothing, he deceiveth himself" (Galatians 6:1-3, KJV).

III. Our Covenant with God

When one makes a covenant with another, everything that one has belongs to the covenant partner. Our covenant with God guarantees us physical protection, protection from our enemies, from the pestilence and from diseases. Because we are in covenant with God through the shed blood of Jesus, we not only have our sins forgiven but everything He has is ours. He Himself is our righteousness. "When you learn to walk as Jesus walked, without consciousness of inferiority to God or Satan, you will have faith that will absolutely stagger the world!" (Kenyon Blood Covenant, 37)

God's Righteousness makes you fearless in Satan's presence. At the very heart of the New Covenant, God makes us like Himself. We are in union with God and become one with Him. "I am the vine you are the branches." Paul said, "It is no longer I that live, but Christ liveth in me."

"Now you can stand as fearlessly in the presence of hell, in the presence of the devil, as you would in the presence of some little inferior thing." (Kenyon Blood Covenant, 38) Jesus was victorious over the devil and conquered him for us.

In the New Covenant, God no longer dwells in a manmade temple. We are the temple of the living God and He lives inside us and greater is He that is in us than He that is in the world. "All of heaven's ability and heaven's glory and heaven's strength are at the disposal of the believer. He has also given us authority to use His name as if He Himself is speaking. It is in the name of Jesus that we cast out the demonic spirits that have strongholds and oppress people.

IV. Commissioned to Deliver and Heal

We are told by Jesus before He was taken up to Heaven to go into all the world and preach the Gospel to every creature. He said that if we believed in Him, one of the signs that would follow us is that we will drive out demons and also lay hands on the sick and they will get well. One reason that we preach the Gospel with signs following is because the Word of God is quick and powerful and sharper than any two-edged sword dividing asunder even the spirit and soul.

As we preach the Gospel, signs will follow because there is power in the Word of God. God will confirm His word with signs following. As we minister on deliverance and healing people, will know that it is God's will that they are healed. They will believe that God does have the power to set them free and heal them. His healing power is for today His healing power is for now. Those that are healed and delivered will give glory to God. He alone is worthy to be praised. All the Glory belongs to God. He is our healer and deliverer.

CHAPTER TEN

Keep Your Eyes on Jesus

As we have seen in this study, the devil or our adversary, often times wants you to look at man as the source of our problems. However, he also wants you to look to man and not to God as our healer and deliverer. Our enemy tries to keep us from knowing the true and living God.

We see this with man at the pool of Bethesda:

Later on, there was a Jewish festival (feast) for which Jesus went up to Jerusalem. Now there is in Jerusalem a pool near the Sheep Gate. This pool in the Hebrew is called Bethesda, having five porches (alcoves, colonnades, doorways). In these lay a great number of sick folk—some blind, some crippled, and some paralyzed (shriveled up)-waiting for the bubbling up of the water. For an angel of the Lord went down at appointed seasons into the pool and moved and stirred up the water; whoever then first, after the stirring up of the water, stepped in was cured of whatever disease with which he was afflicted. There was a certain man there who had suffered with a deep-seated and lingering disorder for thirty-eight years. When Jesus noticed him lying there [helpless], knowing that he had already been a long time in that condition, He said to him," Do you want to become well?" [Are you really in earnest about getting well?] The invalid answered, "Sir, I have nobody when the water is moving to put me into the pool; but while I am trying to come [into it] myself, somebody else steps down ahead of me." Jesus said to him, "Get up! Pick up your bed (sleeping pad) and walk!" Instantly the man became well and recovered his strength and picked up his bed and walked. But that happened on the Sabbath.

John 5:1-9 (KJV)

Pool of Bethesda - There was a great multitude of blind and maimed people. At a certain season, an angel of the Lord would come and trouble the water and whoever stepped in first was made whole of whatever disease he had.

Jesus arrives and walked up to a man that was powerless to help himself for thirty-eight years, paralyzed, and Jesus asked him a question "Wilt thou be made whole?" He answered Him, "I have no man to help me, when the water is troubled to put me in the pool." Jesus answered him, "Rise take up your bed and walk!" And immediately the man was made whole and took up his bed and walked. In reality, Jesus was saying "I am your man".

Why with a great multitude of people that were sick, did Jesus only heal the one person? Why others around this man didn't shout out to Jesus and ask Him to come and heal them as He had healed this man. The reason the others were not healed, was because they had a man to help them get into the pool. They were so busy looking to their man, they missed their miracle. Their miracle came into the midst of them and left. They were untouched because they were too focused on the natural realm to see God's power manifested right in front of them. (Howard-Browne *How to Increase the Anointing*, 18)

Looking for a man for Finances

Looking for a man for Healing

Looking for a man for Deliverance

Looking for well-known Pastor to receive healing, "If I could just get to that crusade meeting, then I could ..."

Looking to government for help with finances, food, etc.

"If I could just get to that well-known evangelist to pray for me, then I know I would receive deliverance." Putting their trust in man and not directly to God the source of the healing.

We know in Psalms 121 and verse 8 the "The Lord will keep you from all evil; He will keep your life. The Lord will keep your going out and your coming in from this time forth and forevermore."

God is Love. Love Him. Follow His Word, His ways and He will deliver you from all evil, He is the healer.

I. Iniquity - Bondage and Open Doors

God is a God of love, mercy, and grace. His love toward us, toward everyone is unconditional. He gives us time to repent for wrongdoing, sin, and iniquity. He will speak to the hearts of men and guide them in His Word.

However, often times when people have been wronged, wounded, victims of horrible things.... God will speak to the person that has been a victim to forgive the person that has done the evil deed. He will speak to their hearts to love their enemies, bless those that persecute them and do them wrong, bless those that have injured them. But, many will choose to ignore the voice of God and hold resentment, unforgiveness, bitterness in their hearts.

They choose to curse instead of bless, to hate and gossip about the other person, to make sure everyone knows that that person has done something wrong, or is wicked, evil, and purposely try to destroy their reputation and cause division, even at the point of dividing the church and the house of God.

They don't even care to destroy and divide a church just so that they get their say. God says vengeance is His, He will repay.

If we try to take matters into our own hands, judge and pass sentence and pay back and return evil (gossiping, backbiting, et.), this is also a dangerous place to be in. Now this causes the victim, him or herself to be in sin, and iniquity, and also acting as judge.

In the Old Testament, a sin was any act of disobedience against the law of God. However, iniquity was a higher level of sin, in that a person could be overcome by a temptation that caused him to fall into a sin (1 John 2:1, KJV), but iniquity was a willful and premeditated transgression of God's commands. Iniquity is the level of continual sinning that eventually leads to a lifestyle of disobedience. (Stone, *Exposing Satan's Playbook*, 193)

The person chooses not to obey the Holy Spirit speaking to them to love and forgive, the love of God has grown cold and often times until they no longer hear Him speaking to them at all. Much of this is happening in the church today and the Bible tells us that in the last days, "iniquity shall abound" (or increase) prior to the return of Christ.

The iniquity in the heart could cause the "love of many to wax cold" (Matthew 24:12, KJV). Iniquity will eventually take the fire out of your love. Love is the key, right living with God, it is also a key to the Kingdom that Jesus gave us to overcome our enemy and demonic forces.

The end-time spiritual powers work through the iniquity that is increasing in our world today. Demonic spirits can be resisted and rebuked, but the source must be cut off to prevent further bondage. This is closing the door and cutting off any spirit's ability to feed off the sin or negative actions of a person. (Stone, *Exposing Satan's Playbook*, 194)

Sin and iniquity most certainly will impact your prayer life as we read: "If I regard iniquity in my heart the Lord will not hear" (Psalms 66:18, NLV). In reading the New Testament approach to prayer the one thing that does and will hinder your prayer life is your lack of confidence in your prayer through a spirit of condemnation. We read:

My little children let us not love in word or speech but in truth. And by this we know that we are of the truth and shall assure our heart before Him. For if our heart condemns us, God is greater than our hearts and knows all things. Beloved, if our heart does not condemn us, we have confidence toward God. And whatever we ask we receive from Him because we keep His Commandments and do those things that are pleasing in His sight.

I John 3:18 (KJV)

When you sin, there will be a sense of conviction where the Holy Spirit will arrest and seize your attention to call you to repentance. If you obey and repent you will be released from condemnation, which, in Greek thought, is a sentence passed upon a person who was found guilty of a crime. Thus, conviction is the arrest and condemnation is the penalty for the unrepentant sin. If a person's heart senses condemnation when he prays because of a known or hidden sin. Then he has no confidence in his prayer. This may be why many believers always desire someone else to pray for them and their specific needs. They have little confidence in their own prayers.

If someone is engaged in any type of activity in which they always have a feeling of conviction then their prayers will be hindered, as the conviction is a sign of some form of disobedience in your life. If someone is making every effort to be free from things that are a spiritual hinderance, then the grace and mercy of God will be extended to them, even in the midst of their struggle, as God's will is for people to be free. (Stone, *Exposing Satan's Playbook*, 210)

Not everything is a curse. Christ has redeemed us from the curse of the law, being made a curse for us. For it is written cursed is everyone that hangs on a tree. "Why then do we still have curses in our lives? It is because, though Jesus Christ paid for these penalties, we are not appropriating the blessing now made available through the cross."

What does appropriating mean? It means I must obey His commands, so He can honor His Word in my life. It means I must break alliance with any ways of the enemy that I am in agreement with, such as the spirit of fear. (2 Timothy 1:7, KJV).

God honors His Word, but if I am not living by His Word in my life, then He cannot honor His Word in those circumstances. If someone continues to choose to live in fear, one of the practical results is that in the labor process, he will have a physiological response of tensed up muscles, which according to medical research sets up the body for a more difficult labor process. Understanding this you must choose to spiritually labor to enter into that rest. (Wright, *More Excellent Way*, 469). "Let us labor to enter into that rest" (Hebrews 4:11 KJV).

CHAPTER ELEVEN

Love and Healing

When we submit to the Word of God, it absolutely straightens out your mind, and you become more spiritually correct. When you allow yourself to be spiritually corrected by the Word, then your mind can be renewed by the powerful, washing of the water, that is the Word. This renewal takes place within your spirit, not just your mind, and as a result unites in faith with what God already said. When the yielding to the Word takes place, your mind, your soul, and your spirit have become one in obedience to God and your thinking is no longer double minded.

"A double minded man is unstable in all his ways"
James 1:8, KJV

The Bible tells us to be single-minded, having the mind of Christ. Actively engage with God and put on the mind of Christ which is the Word of God. We have the mind of Christ (I Corinthians 2:16, KJV). It is evident throughout the Word of God the importance that God has that we love greatly, that we should love God, love people and love our selves. It is so important that He made it the new commandment that sums up ALL the other commandments.

Love is vital to walking our life in a way that is pleasing to God. We will be single minded and living our lives in obedience to His Word. Sometimes, this is why people are not healed if they are not living their life according to the Word of God, where they love everyone and that includes those that have hurt them or wounded them.

We gain knowledge from the Word, then use the wisdom and apply the Word to our lives. Without the application of God's principles and His ways, we cannot move forward into the wholeness of life that God has prepared for us. We have to appropriate them through obedience. We must desire to grow and be more like our Heavenly Father.

God has set standards in the scripture against the enemy. If we come into agreement with God's ways, the enemy has no right to access us in that area. The enemy can only have access to our lives in places he's been allowed to do so either through generational mindsets that we have inherited or through our own unwillingness to follow God's ways in an area of our lives.

"As the bird by wandering, and the swallow by flying the curse causeless shall not come (Proverbs 26:2, KJV). If someone has a desire to be healed and also walk in the fullness of life that God has prepared for them, he needs to be diligent to understand where the enemy may have gained a foothold in his life. Then he can come out of agreement with him, the enemy, and pursue the Father's heart instead.

I. Unforgiveness - A Block to Deliverance

There can be many different blocks to healing but they all have to do with living a life of love and godliness. Godliness meaning like God and God is love. The number one block to not receiving healing is unforgiveness. There are people that have had many ministers lay hands on them that have strong gifting and anointings for healing and miracles, yet they have not received their healing. Many times, they are holding unforgiveness toward someone that has wounded their soul in some way. They usually think they have a right to have these bad feelings toward the person that has wronged them in some way, and maybe they were sinned against terribly, however, God said, "And whenever you stand praying, if you have anything against anyone forgive him and let it go in order that your Father in Heaven may also forgive you" (Mark 11:25, KJV). It is clear if we are going to pray for something this area of our life must be dealt with and forgiveness must take place in order for our prayers to be answered. Otherwise, we still have sin in our lives.

Forgiveness is important to God; it is part of His nature and an essential component of how He deals with us. What He desires for us, as His children whom He has already forgiven and separated from our sins is that we give the same courtesy to our brothers.

God sees our sin and He sees us separate from the sin that dwells in us. That is what we call separation, the ability to see the sin and hate it, but still see the person and love them despite what might be manifesting through them, knowing that manifestation is not them anyways.

If you forgive them, He will forgive you. If you will have mercy on others, He will have mercy on you. But if you repay evil for evil through unforgiveness, you have separated yourself from Him and chosen to separate yourself from Him and not act according to His nature or represent Him in the earth.

Unforgiveness is a dangerous trap spread out for us to keep us bound to the evil of the past and unable to move forward into freedom. It will recall and replay a person's offenses against us over and over again and keep us stuck in bondage to it. It has been likened to a person eating rat poison and expecting the rat to die. It is actually detriment to our own health and freedom.

When we choose to release another person from their offenses against us we are placing them in God's hands. We are removing ourselves from what they did against us and moving on. The Word teaches us further how we are to treat our enemies:

But I say unto you, love your enemies, bless those that curse you, do good to those that hate you, and pray for them which despitefully use you, and persecute you. That ye may be the children of your Father which is in heaven: for He makes His sun to rise on the evil and the good and sends rain on the just and the unjust. For if you love them that love you what reward do you have? Do not even the publicans the same? And if you salute your brethren only, what do you more [than others]? Do not even the publicans do so? Be ye therefore perfect, even as your Father which is in heaven is perfect.
Matthew 5:44-48 (AMP)

When we forgive and submit a person to God in prayer, He can actually change our heart for that person and give us a compassion that was otherwise impossible before. This is liberty! This is a captive being set free, total freedom and forgiveness, we forgive, and we are forgiven. The door to the enemy is closed.

The perfection referred to in Matthew Chapter 5 verse 48, is the perfecting of our hearts in forgiveness toward others as we become more like our Father in

Heaven. Love is the completeness of God's nature. If we want to be more like Him, we need to be love too. God loved us while we were still sinners and He ask us to represent that love to those around us. That love is the ultimate testimony of our faith. "By this shall all men know that you are my disciples if you have love one to another" (John 13:35, KJV).

We must repent and ask God to forgive us for having the emotion of unforgiveness toward that person. We must be at peace with everyone, at peace with God, and peace with ourselves. If this seems too difficult, we ask God to help us to forgive and love and to turn our hearts. Even though you are releasing them from their offenses the person that really gains freedom is the one that forgives.

We forgive as an act of obedience to our Heavenly Father, because we love Him and want to be more like Him. We have the Holy Spirit in us, and He will give us the power to overcome (*Be in Health*, Blog June 14, 2018).

II. All the Promises are Yes and Amen - But

all the promises of God are yes and in Him amen, unto the Glory of God, by us.

2 Corinthians 1:20 (KJV)

But there are conditions for the promises. In the Bible, we find the words if, then, and but. We have to appropriate them through our obedience, which is better than sacrifice. With freedom comes a great responsibility. Freedom requires an effort. The Bible says, "Submit to God resist the devil and he will flee from you." God does the work in us, but he requires our participation.

For I have no pleasure in the death of him that dieth, saith the Lord God: wherefore turn yourselves, and live ye.

Ezekiel 18:32 (KJV)

The Lord is not slack concerning His promise, as some men count slackness; but is long-suffering to us-ward, not willing that any should perish, but that all should come to repentance.

2 Peter 3:9 (KJV)

Having therefore these promises, dearly beloved, let us cleanse ourselves from all filthiness of the flesh and the spirit, perfecting holiness in the fear of God.

II Corinthians 7:1 (KJV)

Seek first the kingdom of God and His righteousness and all these things will be added unto you.

Matthew 6:33 (KJV)

Humble yourselves therefore under the mighty hand of God, that He may exalt you in due time; casting all your care upon Him, for He cares for you. Be sober be vigilant; Because your adversary the devil, as a roaring lion, walks about seeking whom he may devour: Whom resist stedfast in the faith, knowing that the same afflictions are accomplished in your brethren that are in the world.

I Peter 5:6-9 (KJV)

"The work of God in the earth today is one of sanctification. Often you will not receive healing and deliverance from God without first submitting to God" (Wright, More Excellent Way , 48). God tells us to be a doer of the Word, and not a hearer only.

"If we could just get people to walk in love and know what belongs to them because they're walking in love we would't have to have healing services for Christians! We would have them for unbelievers instead." (Hagin, Love Never Fails, 13).

III. Addictions - Root Cause - Unloving Spirit

When sharing the Word of God on any subject such as addictions, it is meant to penetrate the human heart for conviction, not for accusation. Hearts will be opened and freedom from all addictions.

Behind addictions is the need to be loved. Again, we find love or not being loved when deliverance is necessary to set the captive free.

Life can be stressful. It can be filled with trouble or pain that can breed hopelessness and despair. If someone does not know how to deal with these seasons in life, that person can fall prey to addictions. And there are many types of addictions.

Addictions can develop when someone continually attempts to soothe or comfort themselves rather than resolve the source of pain. Addictions are common around the world and is no respecter of persons.

People can become addicted to many things. Some addictions are obvious, some are subtle. Anything you cannot lay down by an act of your will is an addiction. It may be pornography; it might be drugs; it might be an ungodly relationship; it might be food, it might be gossip, it might be television. Addictions are usually associated with such things as alcohol or cocaine. However, any addictions which control you and rules you are your master. IT is your master. The Lord is not your master. Lord means "master of" or "ruler of." Anything that rules you is your master. There is something from within controlling you. (Wright, *Addictions*, 2)

The force behind addiction is rooted in the need to be loved. The need to be loved takes you into a world of finding love in all the wrong places, and that place can include a chemical. The enemy knows how to bind you at this level.

O foolish Galatians, who hath bewitched you that you should not obey the truth, before whose eyes Jesus Christ hath been evidently set forth, crucified among you? This only would I learn of you Received ye the Spirit by the works of the law, or by hearing of faith? Are ye so foolish? Having begun in the Spirit are ye made perfect in the flesh?

Galatians 3:1-3 (KJV)

Verse one asks the question: Who has bewitched you? The foundational root in addiction is spiritual bewitchment. The Gospel is the truth and a very simple gospel. The verse reads that some of the Galatians were bewitched and not obeying the truth or the Gospel.

Jesus said unto him, "Thou shall love the Lord they God with all thy heart, and with all thy soul, and with all thy mind. This is the first and great commandment. And the second is like unto it, thou shalt love thy neighbor as thyself. On these two commandments hang all the law and the prophets."

Matthew 22:37-40 (KJV)

Addictions are rooted in the need to be loved. You stand complete in the Gospel by accepting God's love and receiving the love you need for yourself. Many are believing a lie by thinking that God does not love them. Then you do not love yourself, and you think others do not love you. This means accepting who you are in the new birth once and for all, having quit your arguing with God or anyone else about it, and having love for others.

If you would love God, love yourself, love others, and be complete in that, you would never need to find love in any of the wrong places. However, your enemy knows that if he can get you into a place where you do not feel like you are loved by God, or that you do not love or like yourself and you are not sure about your neighbor, then he can get you to start looking for an outside "fix."

When you do not love yourself or when you do not accept who you are, the first thing that happens in your body chemistry is a dip in your serotonin levels. Serotonin is a neurotransmitter that is released out of the nervous system, out of the dendrites, or in the basil ganglia, which is part of your brain stem. Serotonin is referred to as a "feel good" hormone because it makes you "feel good."

Your enemy knows there is a mind-body connection and that by manipulating your thoughts, he can cause your body to under-secrete serotonin. He knows the hypothalamus and brainstem assist in regulating serotonin levels in the body.

If you start stewing in your juices about God, yourself, or others, and if you are not feeling loved in any area, he can use that hypothalamus/brainstem connection to make your serotonin levels drop. When you have a serotonin deficiency, you will not feel right physically or spiritually. Then you are really in trouble.

If you take your peace with God, yourself and others, the hypothalamus will recognize your fulfillment and signal the brainstem to release and increase serotonin values. This causes your spirit and your body to come into balance again, so you feel more complete.

Peace I leave with you, my peace I give unto you; not as the world giveth, give I unto you. Let not your heart be troubled, neither let it be afraid.

John 14:27, KJV)

When we find addictions, we invariably find a person who is separated from God, separated from himself, and/or separated from others. That person is separated from love. We find this every single time. When someone is struggling with addiction, that person has been spiritually bewitched away from the simplicity of the Gospel, which is love. They are not mixing their new birth with faith by accepting God, themselves, or others in love. That is the foundational root of all addictions.

When someone stays angry or upset, their serotonin levels become deficient. The enemy knows there is no way you can increase serotonin levels unless you take a drug because you are in chemical imbalance. Now enters the sorcerer, otherwise known as your friendly neighborhood pharmacist. The person is given a serotonin enhancer (drug) to make them feel good. They become addicted to the drug which serves to create a chemically altered state of consciousness or false peace. However, the person still has an unloving spirit. The peace is not the peace Jesus gives. The person may not feel satisfied, just more tormented. It is a counterfeit fulfillment. (Wright, *Addictions*,10)

It will be difficult to walk away from your addictions while still feeling unloved. When you try, there is something that is called cross addiction. Where you lay one addiction down and pickup another addiction.

You can recognize this spiritual bewitchment. What is the spiritual bewitchment? You are listening to the lie that you are not loved by God. You are listening to a lie that you do not belong on this planet and you do not love yourself. You are listening to a lie that others do not love you. If they do not love you, that is their loss, but you do not have to carry someone else sin in your body for your destruction. (Wright, *Addictions*, 18)

CHAPTER TWELVE

What to Do When You Have Been Wronged?

Follow the Actions of Christ - What a True Disciple Should Do

One of the most amazing demonstrations of love is what Jesus did knowing Judas was going to betray Him. A betrayal that would cause such brutal, physical torture, beatings, whippings that would rip His flesh apart, His beard being plucked out, a crown of long thorns pressed into His head, long nails being hammered into the left hand, nails hammered into His right hand, nails hammered into His feet, a sword that would pierce His side. A very bloody torture, and mental anguish. He was spit upon by many people, laughed at and mocked during His suffering and His clothes were taken from Him. Publicly, displayed for all to see His wounds.

This betrayal was by His close friend whom He loved, that sat at the table and ate with Him daily. The one He entrusted with the finances. We know that Jesus came to lay down His life for us, a ransom for us, but the one that betrayed Him, caused the killers to come and take Him to His death.

Jesus knowing Judas was going to betray him still washed Judas feet! He still ate and drank with him, gave bread, and had meals together. And after the terrible suffering on the cross and He had risen from the dead, Jesus ran into two disciples on the road to Emmaus, they did not recognize Jesus but were talking about all the things that had happened to Jesus. When Jesus asked, "What are you discussing about?" The two said, "Are you alone? Do you not know what has happened these days with Jesus of Nazareth?" And they went on to tell all the terrible things He had suffered. And Jesus replied, "What things?" He already let go of any bad feelings toward Judas. He did not have anger, unforgiveness, bitterness toward Judas. He did not try to talk bad about Judas and agree with how terrible he was or let the world know what He went through and point out who His betrayer was.

James 1:22 says, we are to be doers of the Word and not just listeners to it. Follow His example and clean wash dirty feet, and forgive those that have hurt us, betrayed us, physically wounded us, emotionally abused us.

When we have been wronged, we must allow the Word of God and His promptings to govern our lives. We must not react and go by our feelings of hurt, pain, disappointments and allow ourselves to become wounded and think of ourselves as victims. When the hurt rises up, we must deal with those things. We must remove the pain and hurt. The way we do that is to forgive and trust Jesus. We must be mature enough to walk through it for the sake of Christ Jesus. To forgive when no one is asking. To trust that the head of the Church knows what He is doing when He ask us to release the person that has wounded us.

Psalms 73:1 says when there is an ache inside that you cannot express in words, the pain that is deep in your heart, you must believe in God and do what is right. Get out of the snare of the enemy; obey Jesus no matter the cost or the price. No matter the memory or pain continue to love God and love people. You can find fault in people and reasons not to love people, but don't let humanity and situations disconnect you from the divine where God has placed you (venom in your voice about the wrong that has been done to you.)

Churches split, families divide, marriages shatter, and love dies, crushed by an onslaught of words launched in hurt and frustration. Offended by friends, family, and leaders, we take aim with words sharpened by bitterness and anger. Even though information may be factual and accurate, motives are impure. (Bevere, *Bait of Satan*, 39).

Proverbs 6:16-19 says that sowing discord or separation among brethren is an abomination to the Lord. When we repeat something with the intention of separating or damaging relationships or reputations- even though it is true - it is still an affront to God.

Another Biblical example of someone returning evil for good is the story of David and Saul. Even though Saul attempted many times to kill David and had many innocent people killed because he thought they were helping David. David refused to avenge himself in this situation. David left him in God's hand to judge. How many people today have a heart like David's? We no longer kill with physical swords but ravage each other with a sword of another kind - the tongue. "Death and life are in the power of the tongue" (Proverbs 18:21, KJV).

David chose to let God be Saul's judge. Saul died battling the Philistines. David did not celebrate instead, he mourned. He asked the people to sing in honor of Saul. He called for all of Israel to weep over Saul. This is not the heart of an offended man. An offended man would have said, "He got what he deserved!" David went even further He did not kill the remaining seed of the house of Saul. Instead he showed kindness to them. He gave land and food to them and granted a descendant a seat at the kings table. Does this sound like an offended man? Even though David was rejected by the one who should have fathered him, he remained loyal even after Saul's death. It is easy to be loyal to a leader or father who loves you, but what about one who is out to destroy you? Will you be a man or woman after the heart of God, or will you seek to avenge yourself? (Bevere, *Bait of Satan*, 43).

"Beloved, do not avenge yourselves, but rather give place to wrath; for it is written, 'Vengeance is Mine, I will repay,' says the Lord" (Romans 12:19, KJV). It is righteous for God to avenge His servants. It is unrighteous for God's servants to avenge themselves. Many today that become offended will treat others dishonorably and do whatever it takes to make them pay for the offense not seeing their own character flaws such as allowing offense.

CHAPTER THIRTEEN

Love, the New Commandment

Jesus said, "A new commandment I give unto you. Love one another as I have loved you. That ye love one another. By this all men shall know that you are My disciples, if you have love one to another."

John 13:34-35, KJV

This is the way people will know if we are His disciples, we will have love for one another.

The new law of love took place of the old law, or old ten commandments. Jesus fulfilled the old covenant and established the new covenant in His blood. And there is no need for Ten Commandments now for us who are in Christ. In the book of Romans chapter thirteen it explains, if we walk in love, we have fulfilled the law. If we walk in love, there is no need for the ten commandments now for us who are in Christ. We will not break any of the Ten Commandments against sin. If we love one another, we will not steal from them, will not want to hurt, ... (Love works no ill to his neighbor). Walk in the new commandment to love.

Ezekiel and Jeremiah both prophesied and referred to the new covenant. Hebrews 8:6, "Now hath He obtained a more excellent ministry (previously was talking about Moses and the priesthood) by how much more also He is the mediator of better covenant." He said I will make a new covenant when I brought them out of the land of Egypt. (the New Testament is the new covenant). I will put (give) my laws in their minds, (He gave us the New Testament we can read it and He has given us a new covenant in our mind) I will write them in their heart. The old commandment is written with the finger of God (the Holy Spirit), now it is written in our spirits.

It is written in the love of God, as we can see in Romans 5:5, "The love of God is shed abroad in our hearts (our spirits) through the Holy Spirit Who has been given to us" in our hearts or inner man. God is love. The God kind of love is in our hearts. We must listen to our hearts. The law, it is written in our hearts.

Galatians 5:14, "For ALL the law is fulfilled in one word, even in this, thou shalt love thy neighbor as thy self." If you love your neighbor, you have fulfilled the whole law and you will not need to remember any other commandment.

We read in Galatians 5:22, "But, the fruit of the spirit is love, joy, peace, patience, kindness, goodness, faithfulness, gentleness, self-control. Against such there is no law."

The word 'spirit' in the Greek language is *pnuema* and has only one word for spirit.

The first fruit of a born-again child of God is love. Jesus said in John 15, "I am the vine; My Father is the husbandman. Every branch that does not bear fruit, My Father cuts down. Now you are clean according to the Word."

"I am the vine you are the branches." Fruit grows on the branch, because of life that comes out of the trunk or branch, because the life of Christ within us. Because we are connected to God.

"We know that we have passed from death unto life, (from spiritual death to eternal life)" (I John 3:14, KJV). That means we have been born again; we have become the children of God; we know, because we love the brethren.

The first fruit is love, of the born-again spirit because of the life of Christ within, and that love is in our heart and in our spirit. Ephesians 4:32, "Be ye kind, tenderhearted to one another." We must be tender hearted. If He told us to do it, that means we can do it. That also means forgiving one another, even as God forgives. Love and forgiveness go hand in hand. We can forgive even as God forgives because the same kind of love of God is shed abroad in our hearts, in our spirit by the Holy Spirit.

How does God forgive? He said, "I, even I, am He that blotteth out thy transgressions and I will not remember your iniquities" (Isaiah 43:25, KJV). That is the way God forgives, and that is the way He wants us to forgive. And if we walk in love that is the way we will forgive. This is how we are to be. You will not keep reminding people of what they did to you. Don't bring up the past, or remind them of what they did, of past mistakes, and sins and failures. Forget the sin, and when the devil tries to bring it up, laugh and say, "It happened, but I forgive them." Love and forgiveness go hand in hand.

Mark 11:23-24 reads, "Whosoever shall say unto this mountain be thou removed and cast into the sea, and shall not doubt in his heart but believe that you receive them and you shall have whatsoever you say." Then the very next words of Jesus are, "And when ye stand praying forgive, if you have (ought) anything against anyone." Anything means anything, little, big or middle sized. Jesus said if you have anything against anyone. In the Old Testament, it is the little foxes that spoil the vine. The little things that you don't think matter too much, can spoil the vine, can keep you from receiving your healing, can keep you from receiving the blessings of God. The Bible also says can keep you from receiving your prayers from being answered because the Bible also says, that "Faith works by love" (Galatians 5:6, KJV).

If I [can] speak in the tongues of men and [even] of angels, but have not love (that   reasoning, intentional, spiritual devotion such as is inspired by God's love for and in us), I am only a noisy gong or a clanging cymbal.

I Corinthians 13:1 (AMP)

When we walk in love, we can claim the promises of God and receive them because we are walking in love. Under the old commandment, God said, "Keep my statutes and walk in My ways and do that which is right in My sight and I will not put any of these diseases upon you."

"If thou will diligently hearken to the voice of the Lord your God, I will not put any of these disease upon you" (Exodus 15:26, KJV). It looks like from this He will put diseases on you. But, in the original language it is a permissive which reads, "Will not allow these plagues to come upon you." He may permit evil but not create evil nor commit evil. There is a difference between commission and permission.

Also, in Amos 3:6, "Shall a trumpet be blown in the city and the people not be afraid? If a disaster or misfortune occurs in a city has not the Lord caused it?"

The correct translation is *allowed* instead of the word caused.

In I Samuel 16:15, "The Spirit of the Lord departed Saul and an evil spirit from the Lord troubled him." Should be translated in the permissive sense in that He "permits." If evil spirits come from God, we should not resist them, but they do not come from God.

In I Samuel 16:15 (as mentioned above) an evil spirit troubled Saul. Saul's sin broke fellowship with God, and God allowed the evil spirit to trouble him. Original Hebrew should have been translated from the permissive sense. God does not send sickness upon His people. Again, God does NOT send sickness upon His people. God's word teaches us sickness comes from Satan.

"How God anointed Jesus of Nazareth with the Holy Spirit and with power and went about doing good and healing all that were oppressed of the devil for God was with Him."

Acts 10:38 (KJV)

These people broke His commandments and when they did they were out from under His divine protection; they couldn't claim His protection anymore. All God could do is permit the devil to bring these afflictions upon them; their sin and wrongdoing was the thing that brought the sickness and plagues to come upon them. "But if you keep My commandments, I will take the sickness from thee for I am the Lord that healeth thee" (Exodus 15:26, KJV).

The illustration of a child that you tell, "Don't touch that burner or you will get burned!" You turn around and they touch it anyway; they scream and get burned. You didn't make them do it. They have a will. You did not want to teach the child that way, but they have a free will. It is the same thing with sin. If you tell people what will happen if you sin and if they want to do it and go and do it anyway, God is telling them what will happen if they do it. It may not be your way of teaching the child that a hot skillet will burn, it is not that you are that cruel. And that is not Gods way of teaching you and putting sickness on you if you sin. That is not love. He allowed the consequences because you have a free will, and you did the sin anyway. Sickness and disease are not of love. God is love. We need to see that. *"I am the Lord that healeth thee."*

You shall serve the Lord your God; He shall bless your bread and water, and I will take sickness from your midst. None shall lose her young by miscarriage or be barren in your land; I will fulfill the number of your days.

Exodus 23:25-26 (KJV)

If sickness was taken away, they would NOT get sick. The number of thy days I will fulfill. Deuteronomy 7:15,

"And the Lord will take away from thee ALL sickness and will not allow any evil diseases of Egypt to come on you."

They had the potential of living out days of living without ever getting sickness and disease and fulfill the number of their days. The possibility existed to live and not even get sick to die. They could just fulfill the number of their days. In Hebrews Chapter 8, we see that we have a "Better covenant established on better promises." Now we have a better covenant.

"Owe no man anything but to love one another" (Romans 13, KJV). It is not talking about not buying anything on credit; no, you should pay your bills - your house, or something on credit. You pay your water bill on credit, your light bill on credit. You are not in debt unless you don't pay debt; then you are in debt. The debt to love one another will never be paid. Keep loving.

"He that loveth another has fulfilled the law" (Romans 13:8, KJV). In the Old Covenant God said, "Keep may statues and obey My commandments and I will not allow any of these diseases to come on you." So, if we fulfill the law, we will get the blessing. If we don't obey the commandments, then the curses will come on us. We must declare every day and say, "I will, and I do walk in love." Jesus came, died, and rose again and gave us the new commandment to love. Romans 13:9, "For this Thou shalt not commit adultery, thou shalt

not steal, ...bear false witness... and if there be any other commandment, it is briefly comprehended in this saying namely thou shalt love they neighbor as thyself."
Verse 10: "Love worketh no ill to his neighbor. Therefore, love is the fulfilling of the law."

If we walk in love, we have fulfilled the law. Then the blessing should be ours. If we do not walk in love and obey the commandment to love, then the curses can come; because if we don't obey the voice of God or His Word, then Deuteronomy says the curses will come upon the those that are not obedient to walk in love. You have to claim the blessing. The new commandment to love fulfills all the old law.

The New Birth, the remission of sin, belongs to all sinners but some don't have it because some people don't know about it. Some know about it, and don't accept it, and have even rejected it. God said in His Word, "My people perish for lack of knowledge" (Hosea 4:6, KJV). If they don't know, Satan takes advantage of them.

For all the law is fulfilled in this that Thou shalt love thy neighbor as thy self.
Galatians 5:14 (KJV).

Every step out of love is sin. If you get out of love, get right back in it quickly as you can so the enemy has no legal authority in your life. There will not be an open door to the enemy in your life.

As I said earlier, faith works by love (Galatians 5:6, KJV). You can have a lot of faith, but other people hold you back because they do not have enough faith. When they sent the spies out, Joshua and Caleb had the faith to enter but others didn't, and it took forty years because the others held them back.

Some of the characteristics of love is to be quick to repent, quick to forgive, and quick to believe. Love and forgiveness go hand in hand. When we walk in love we will want to forgive.

We are born again and born of God. God is love and we are born of love. We must purpose in our hearts to walk in love, talk in love, and act in love. And live free of sickness and disease. Live out our full length of time here on earth without sickness and disease and just fall asleep in Jesus.

CHAPTER FOURTEEN

Sickness and Walking Out of Love

Sickness and Walking in Love

Godly order in the home is important. The man was intended to represent Father God in the home; his responsibility is to establish the spiritual and emotional welfare of the home. The home needs to be a place of nurturing, love, stability and safety for all of its inhabitants. Understanding Godly order is very important in overcoming many sicknesses including fibromyalgia. This sickness seems to be more and more common over the years.

But I would have you know that the head of every man is Christ; and the head of the woman [is] the man; and the head of Christ [is] God.

I Corinthians 3:11 (KJV)

The woman was created to be a follower of good, strong, Godly leadership. That's what the Bible teaches. It says that the man wasn't made for the woman, but the woman for the man. That does not give the man the right to become chauvinistic. It means he has a tremendous responsibility to take care of what God gave him.

Husbands and wives were created to complement one another in the government of the home. They each bring a dimension of who God is. One does not have more value than the other; they just have different roles according to how God designed them.

There is neither Jew nor Greek, there is neither bond nor free, there is neither male nor female: for ye are all one in Christ Jesus.

Galatians 3:28 (KJV)

So, what happens when the family isn't functioning the way God designed it to? What happens when the head of the home doesn't know how to be a source of love, peace and safety for those under his roof? What happens when the wife doesn't know how to let her husband cover her? The door may be open to the enemy to come in and bring torment and fear and eventually disease.

"There is no fear in love; but perfect love casteth out fear: because fear hath torment. He that feareth is not made perfect in love."

1 John 4:18 KJV (KJV)

Fibromyalgia is a prime example of this dynamic. Statistics show that 99% of those suffering from fibromyalgia are female. According to the Merck manual (a Doctor's handbook), fibromyalgia is a non-inflammatory syndrome that involves pain in the fibrous tissues, muscles, tendons, ligaments and other 'white' connective tissues. It often involves constant pain with no biological reason. The medical community has identified it as primarily a fear and stress-based disease. In fact, the Merck Manual says, "Primary Fibromyalgia Syndrome is particularly likely to occur in healthy young women who tend to be stressed, tense, depressed, anxious, and striving." There is a strong connection between fibromyalgia, chronic fatigue syndrome, MCS/EI and depression. But even with this information, their ability to treat it is limited mostly to medications and therapies intended to manage the symptoms, with no hope of a long-term fix. (Wright, *More Excellent Way*, 90)

According to observations, the reason that fibromyalgia is primarily a female disease is because females seem to be more susceptible to anxiety at this level than males. From his investigation, Dr. Henry Wright considers fibromyalgia to be the result of separation of a woman from Godly male leadership and covering that should be there. Because that is missing, abandonment issues surface, and insecurity and fear come because they don't feel properly cared for or nurtured.

When we look deeper into exactly how fear and stress affect the body, we can understand exactly what is happening. Fear affects the entire physiological and neurological and chemical makeup of our bodies. When we are in fear or stress, various chemicals are released into our bodies by the hypothalamus. These chemicals were designed by God to put our bodies into fight or flight mode in the case of a dangerous situation so that we can react and protect ourselves. When a person struggles with long term stress, these chemicals and hormones continue to course through their body and begin to cause malfunction, imbalance, and even damage to certain organs and body systems.

In the case of fibromyalgia, these stress hormones trigger the nervous system to misfire. Normally, when you think to move your arm, your brain will send a signal through your nervous system, from your nerves to your muscles, to trigger the desired response. Nerve signals are also released to cause things like heartbeats, blinking and breathing to automatically function without conscious thought to keep your body alive. A nerve cell can be visualized like an arm or multiple arms with fingers at the end of each arm called dendrites. At the dendrite's tip is something called a nerve synapse. This is the exchange point between the nerve cells. The nerve cells don't actually touch but are surrounded by a fluid that can conduct the electrical or chemical signal being sent from nerve to nerve.

Behind the scenes, fear, anxiety, and stress are operating to produce a thought that can be beyond our consciousness. We may feel its presence and call it an emotion or intuitive insight. It may cause uneasiness. It can be subtle or very obvious. But the master gland of the endocrine system, the hypothalamus, will recognize that thought. It will then manufacture various different hormones that have direct access to the central nervous system. As the fear, anxiety and uneasiness grows in power, there is a nerve impulse that is released by the hypothalamus beyond the realm of consciousness. It travels down the nerve into the dendrite but there is no corresponding action. It will not connect across the nerve synapse to the receptor that would normally cause a muscle response. Instead it will pulsate at the nerve ending and cause the pain of fibromyalgia.

That is why fibromyalgia is considered to be the result of fear, anxiety, and stress. This stress may come when a person feels driven or pressure to perform. They may spend their whole life trying to meet the expectations of others. Perhaps they were abandoned in love or not even loved at all. There may be many door points in a person's life and circumstances and even in family trees. And with all of that comes the torment that we see in 1 John 4:18, "Fear has torment." That torment is what sets into motion the mind-body connection and the various physiological responses.

Fear is considered by most ministers and especially those involved with deliverance ministry to be a spiritual problem, not just a psychological problem. The Word says this: "For God hath not given us the spirit of fear; but of power, and of love, and of a sound mind" (2 Timothy 1:7, KJV).

And again in Romans it says, "For ye have not received the spirit of bondage again to fear; but ye have received the spirit of adoption, whereby we cry, Abba, Father" (Romans 8:15, KJV).

As a child of God, we have the opportunity to embrace everything good that He would offer us in spite of the failures of others. When we have peace with God, what is there to be afraid of? He has promised in His Word that He would never leave us or forsake us (Hebrews 13:5, KJV). He will cover us and protect us (Psalms 91:4, KJV). He will provide for all our needs (Matthew 6:31-32, KJV). He wants to give us and grant us the desires of our heart (Psalms 37:4, KJV), and He wants good for us and not evil (Jeremiah 29:11, KJV). That is love;

that is the perfection of love because God is love (1 John 4:16, KJV).

The choice rests in our hands; will we choose to believe God's promises, or will we choose to believe the evil that the enemy projects from our pasts into our futures? When we defeat the enemy of fear in our lives, and come to trust and receive the love of our Heavenly Father and learn to rest in that place of hope and peace in Father God our body will normalize and come into balance once again and function the way it was created to. Fibromyalgia doesn't stand a chance against this, neither does any other fear and stress related disease.

In teaching on the subject of love and deliverance, many people are completely healed of these diseases because they chose to apply the truth of God's Word into their lives and walk in the wholeness of life that God designed them for them.

CHAPTER FIFTEEN

Fear of Man

Fear is multifaceted and can make its way into almost every area of our life, if we let it. We need to understand how it operates and learn how to recognize it so that we can defeat it. It is devious, its main goal is to separate us from love and trust in God, ourselves, and others.

One of the major areas that fear brings a snare is in the area of relationships, especially through fear of rejection, fear of failure and fear of man. Fear can train us from our earliest existence to expect and dread rejection, to perform for approval and to be afraid of what others may do to us or think about us. It trains us to develop mechanisms of self-protection in order to avoid the pain of these projected realities. It creates a false sense of security and prevents us from recognizing the bondage that we've been placed under and makes us unable to overcome.

For many of us, perhaps the environment we grew up in wasn't a safe place. Maybe we weren't raised feeling loved, nurtured, and secure. Perhaps there was no place of stability. For some of us, no matter what we did, we couldn't seem to win the approval that we so desperately craved. Perhaps we were constantly criticized or corrected, out of control and fear. So we were trained from that time to look to man, to hyper analyze every move we made, to expect the shoe to drop if we messed up, and possibly to be driven to performance and perfectionism in order to receive approval. In short, Father God's love was misrepresented to us.

Before we get all down on our parents or the people that trained us in this, we need to recognize that they may not have known any better or differently. It's highly possible that they were never treated with the proper, unconditional love of God themselves. Perhaps they had a form of love that they thought was right but just missed the mark in some ways. It's important to understand that these behaviors and shortfalls are often passed down from generation to generation as a carefully orchestrated set-up by the enemy.

Fear of man will constantly have you looking to man rather than to God. It will try to seek man's approval continually. It's actually a form of idolatry because it can lead a person to be more concerned with what man thinks about them than what God thinks. It will make us more concerned about how man treats us than in trusting God to protect us.

Fear of man may drive every decision, every action and motivation through a filter of what others will think or do. It may lead to withdrawal if a person comes to the realization that they can never measure up or feels like they cannot get it right, or will always be mistreated, they may just try to escape and give up. It can cause isolation. It will come with accusation to convince a person that everyone out there is judging them and thinks they are unworthy or a failure. It will convince a person that their value is wrapped up in what others think.

With fear of man comes fear of failure. Fear of failure provides no room for mistakes or humanness. It will paralyze a person from the ability to make choices or to engage in relationships. It will cause insecurity in decisions and a dread of failing on any and every level. If, by chance, a person does stick their neck out and try something and make a mistake or fail, fear of failure will come with its buddies, accusation, guilt and shame to ensure that they cannot rise up again. These will hold all of that person's failures, past and present over their head and project them into the future with the intent of debilitating that person in fear.

Fear of rejection has its fingers in all of this as well. It accompanies fear of man, and fear of failure. It will cause a person to lose the battle between their ears before they ever get to the war. It'll have a person speculate on who is going to reject them and how they are going to be rejected. It will expect rejection and when accompanied by rejection will cause a person to even demand to be rejected. It will cause a person to be so concerned about whether or not they are accepted or rejected by others that they will be unable to develop their own identity. They will be too fearful to express their own opinion, beliefs or values and often times just find themselves following the herd.

This can all boil down to one question: Who is your source?

The breakdown in relationship between God, we, and others is the root of 80% of all diseases. The enemy knows if he can cause separation at any of these levels, we are easy pickings. Fear will come disguised as a friend or a helper; it will offer us a means of self-protection, security, and perhaps a feeling of being in control. Really, what it is doing is helping us build up walls around our hearts to keep us in and others, even God, out. That's where the separation occurs.

Fear also knows that if it can make others our source, so that we look to them to fulfill our need for approval, acceptance and love, sooner or later they will let us down. After all, they are only human. Then, because we've valued their opinion and treatment of us so highly, we have a lot farther to fall. It can make the hurt and pain of betrayal or the failure of others seem so much more acute. This establishes the territory for bitterness, rejection, unloving, accusation, and more. What is our alternative then?

The Word says, *"The fear of man bringeth a snare: but whoso putteth his trust in the Lord shall be safe."* (Proverbs 29:25, KJV)

God is the only being who will not fail us. He is steadfast and true. He is full of mercy, kindness, and compassion towards us. He is patient with us and He is longsuffering for us. Above all, His love is unconditional; it does not depend on our performance, does not falter in our failures, and even remains strong through every circumstance in life, in sickness and in health, for rich or for poor.

"The Lord is gracious, and full of compassion; slow to anger, and of great mercy."

Psalm 145:8 (KJV)

"It is of the Lord's mercies that we are not consumed, because His compassions fail not. They are new every morning: great is thy faithfulness."

Lamentations 3:22-23 (KJV)

Maybe we were trained by religion to believe that God was the judge and punisher and therefore He became a fearful person instead of a source of love and strength. The enemy can come with accusations, fear, guilt, and shame to convince us that we are unworthy of God's love and don't qualify as His children. So, who are we going to believe? If we continue to believe these lies, we will continue in the bondage and desolation of our generations. Yet the Word says that we were chosen and are accepted by God into His family if we choose to be.

But as many as received Him, to them gave the power to become the sons of God, even to them that believe on His name.

John 1:12 (KJV)

According as he hath chosen us in him before the foundation of the world, that we should be holy and without blame before Him in love: Having predestinated us unto the adoption of children by Jesus Christ to himself, according to the good pleasure of his will, to the praise of the glory of His grace, wherein He hath made us accepted in the beloved.

Ephesians 1:4-6 (KJV)

Overcoming fear requires a choice to believe and receive God's truth over the programmed, familiar lies of the enemy in our lives. This requires searching out His Word in order to understand His heart and His character more fully and intimately. If a person does not believe God's Word, they have a spirit of unbelief. If they are unable to believe God's Word, they may have an antichrist spirit which can be associated with occultism.

Let us therefore come boldly unto the throne of grace, that we may obtain mercy, and find grace to help in time of need.

Hebrews 4:16 (KJV)

Overcoming fear also requires us to take our position as sons and daughters of God and use the authority that He has given to us over the enemy.

Behold, I give unto you power to tread on serpents and scorpions, and over all the power of the enemy: and nothing shall by any means hurt you.

Luke 10:19 (KJV)

Casting down imaginations, and every high thing that exalteth itself against the knowledge of God, and bringing into captivity every thought to the obedience of Christ.

II Corinthians 10:5 (KJV)

When we recognize these dynamics of fear in our life we can now come boldly to the throne of grace and repent to our Father in Heaven for not believing His truth and trusting Him but believing the lies of the enemy. Once we've repented and received our forgiveness, we can command the enemy of fear to leave in Jesus's name.

If we confess our sins, he is faithful and just to forgive us our sins, and to cleanse us from all unrighteousness.
I John 1:9 (KJV)

As far as the east is from the west, so far hath he removed our transgressions from us.
Psalm 103:12 (KJV)

We need to be aware and listen to our thoughts; make sure there is no presence of a spirit of fear in our lives that would try to influence our thoughts and keep us in bondage. New thoughts need to be developed instead meditating on things that make you worried or anxious about things that may happen. We need to get into the Word, renew our minds and cast all of our cares on Him.

Be careful for nothing; but in everything by prayer and supplication with thanksgiving let your requests be made known unto God. And the peace of God, which passeth all understanding, shall keep your hearts and minds through Christ Jesus. Finally, brethren, whatsoever things are true, whatsoever things are honest, whatsoever things are just, whatsoever things are pure, whatsoever things are lovely, whatsoever things are of good report; if there be any virtue, and if there be any praise, think on these things.

Philippians 4:6-8 (KJV)

Fear can be defeated but we need to be diligent and aware of what it looks like, sounds like and feels like so that when we catch ourselves falling into its trap, we can rise out again.

For a just man falleth seven times, and riseth up again.

Proverbs 24:16 (KJV)

At first, it may be a hard battle, but over time, as we continue to practice and walk in truth, we will become stronger and stronger and have better discernment so that its power in our lives can be greatly diminished. Temptation will still come, the enemy isn't one to give up easily, but by the grace of God we will.

CHAPTER SIXTEEN

Do Demons Have Legal Rights?

I was a prison chapel minister in Florida. In my past, I had seen demons cast out of people in church before and knew it was real, and I had read about expelling demons in the Bible. But one day, while in the prison chapel, I had invited two friends of mine to come and minister in the prison that day. Toward the end of the service, I had to walk into the next room for something and I was not gone long at all. When I returned, there was a young man lying in the floor up front and one of my friends, was standing over him praying for him. I walked up saw the young man on the floor and he was in full demonic manifestation; like a spider and then like a snake in such a way that is not humanly possible. God knows this is true whether people believe it or not.

His body lifted and only his feet and tip of his fingers were on the floor. He made quick movements and stop, quick movements, and stop again like a spider would move. Then he fell down flat on his stomach on the floor with his arms straight down his side and his head lifted up. He was moving like a snake, slithering in a way that a human cannot move. He moved forward exactly like a snake does, and he moved fast slivering quickly to the back of the chapel behind the last row. Since that day I have seen many other demonic manifestations while praying for people and many people have been set free by the power of God.

This young man was sitting in the chapel service just like everyone else. But then suddenly this demon that had been secretly tormenting his life started to manifest through him openly. Many times, people are tormented by evil spirits that are in the invisible kingdom.

Not everyone that is oppressed by evil spirits are in prison. In fact, I have cast out more devils outside of the prison walls by those that were in their own private prison that no one knew they were in. Jesus said that He came to "set the captives free" and "heal the broken hearted".

Most people that need deliverance are suffering from a broken heart. A heart that should be full of the love of God, but in fact is void of it, and they don't realize the ramifications of a loveless heart. Their hearts have been wounded in some way by someone. It may have happened at a very young age. Abused by a parent or family member, emotional abuse, verbal abuse, physical abuse, rejection, fear (perfect love casts out fear), jealously (person has not received fully the love of God, so they look for love and acceptance in other people), and many other "issues" that stem from loveless homes.

Although they are the "victims" in many situations the Bible warns us to, "guard our hearts with all diligence for out of it the springs of life flow." In some aspects, our quality of life will be determined by how we guard our hearts. Do not allow, sadness, bitterness, rejection, and unforgiveness in our lives because of what others have done to us. This will be an open door to the demonic in our lives to oppress us and torment lives.

You see, Satan is the accuser of the "brethren" and he goes into the courts of heaven that God talks about in Daniel 7:10, "... the court was seated and the books were opened."

Then I heard a strong (loud) voice in heaven, saying, now it has come the salvation and the power and the kingdom (the dominion, the reign) of our God, and the power (the sovereignty, the authority) of His Christ (the Messiah); for the accuser of our brethren, he who keeps bringing before our God charges against them day and night, has been cast out!
Revelation 12:10 (AMP)

We need to dismantle the legal arguments that allow the powers of darkness to rule. This is where many people miss it when trying to do battle the kingdom of darkness. They need to first find out if and why Satan and his cohorts have a legal right to be in our life. What is it he could be accusing us of in the courts of heaven? If something has not moved in your prayers that are still unanswered and you have had much prayer, there is a legal reason for it.

The devil has a legal right to withstand you. The only thing that will bring an answer or freedom is removing the legal right that the devil has to resist us. Persevering prayer is important but the strategies that God has given us in His Word will make us even more effective.

Thank God, Jesus is our Advocate in the courts of Heaven. We go boldly before His throne of grace and find mercy and grace. Because of what Jesus already did for us at the cross we can approach with confidence.

Seeing then that we have a great High Priest who has passed through the Heavens, Jesus the Son of God let us hold fast our confession. For we do not have a High Priest who cannot sympathize with our weaknesses, but was in all points tempted as we are, yet without sin. Let us therefore come boldly to the throne of grace, that we may obtain mercy and find grace to help in the time of need.

Hebrews 4:14-16 (KJV)

God is faithful to keep His covenant with us. He is a just God. He administers justice into place. God loves justice and hates injustice. When we are before Him, we are to confess our sins.

If we confess our sins, He is faithful and just to forgive us our sins and to cleanse us from all unrighteousness.
I John 1:9 (KJV)

When we meet the legal requirements of confession, God is freed to legally forgive us our sins. Because of what Jesus did for us on the cross, God can now legally forgive and cleanse us when we meet the legal requirement of confession. Repentance is so important. We also need to repent of our words that we speak out of frustration.

But I say to you for every idle word men may speak, they will give account of it in the day of judgment. For by your words you will be justified and by your words you will be condemned.
Matthew 12:36-37 (KJV)

God has given mankind a free will, a freedom of choice, and it is by our own choices that we make that will give the demons the legal right. I use the word demons, plural, more than one because remember once the door is open, he can then bring with him more that are stronger than the first.

Many times, we are on the battlefield trying to fight a spiritual warfare without realizing this conflict is a legal one. We must go before the Lord, first submit to God, make sure we are in right standing with God, no known sin in our lives and repent. After repentance, and every place of rebellion is out of us, then resist the devil and he will flee. The devil no longer has a legal right to stay.

James 4:7 (KJV)

Point to remember:

Jesus was speaking to believers, those that believed in Him when He told them how to be free. Most people may not realize John 8:31-32 is also a scripture about how to receive deliverance for those that are held captive. "So, Jesus said to those Jews who had believed in Him, 'If you abide in My word [hold fast to My teachings and live in accordance with them], you are truly My disciples. And you will know the Truth, and the Truth will set you free."

He said if we live according to His Word, we will be free! So, if He told us to love everyone and love ourselves in His new commandment, that means love will set the captives free.

He said to hate no one, bless those that do you wrong, bless and do not curse, do not return evil for evil. Also, when Jesus was telling the people about the strongman or demon spirit that is in a house or person and because of the armor he can remain until someone stronger comes to strip him of the armor, a woman in the crowd yelled out to Jesus "Blessed is the womb that bore you..." (Luke 11:27, KJV).

But Jesus said, "Blessed rather are those that hear the Word of God and do it."

Again, this is how to stay free from demonic oppression. You see when a person yields to the enemy and obeys him rather than keeping and doing the Word of God, he is giving the strong man armor. We must be a doer of the Word of God. Love Him and obey His commands to be free and to remain free. It is not complicated. Choose to LOVE.

CHAPTER SEVENTEEN

Love is the Key

Love is the key to everything we will need in life. In appropriating our salvation, our healing and our deliverance, love is the key. Love is the key to our relationship and fellowship with God. Love is the key to our relationship and fellowship with others. It is the key to freedom from oppression, and it is key to our own happiness.

Proof that the key of life is love, is written all throughout the Holy Bible, in the old testament as well as the new testament. Thousands of years that the Word of God was written, and one theme remains, one requirement for our lives is love. We are also given warnings with consequences if we choose not to love and we see this in the lives of those we read about them. Proof of how we are to live our life is in God's Holy Word and there are scriptures that contain this vital message of love. God said that His people perish for a lack of knowledge. Love is the essence of the Word.

It is important that everyone reads and studies the Word of God concerning love for himself. Something happens in our spirit as we read it. It will change our lives for forever. Let the love of God abide in you and through you. The real love of God will change you and the love of God in you and working through you will touch and change the lives of others.

God said we are nothing without love. Although we Christians may study certain subjects of the scripture such as prophecy, or about the amazing gifts that God gives us or how to have great faith but often times people overlook what Jesus said was the most important thing in our lives and that is the love of God in us. God said if we have faith to move mountains but have not love we are nothing.

Learning to walk in love is not always easy. It can be difficult if we are walking in the flesh and trying to be spiritual and walk in love simultaneously. We can read the scriptures that we are to love our enemies and smile and think we can do that, but many times there may be certain family members that you have a difficult time showing love and mercy and acts of kindness to, the ones that seem to make life miserable for everyone else by their words or actions. Or those that are repeat offenders, those that have wronged you over and over again. With some it maybe a spouse, that keeps mistreating you, verbally abusive for years and you begin to think they will never change why show love any longer because there is no change, or you start to loose the love for him or her. Questions may arise like why show him love if he does not love me anyway?

Seemingly, things get worse and you may even develop a disdain for the person. Perhaps it was once easy to be respectful and kind when the person was speaking abusive to you and now it may seem more difficult than before to continue to show respect, kindness, to continue with mercy and grace and love the person.

God is the same yesterday today and forever. We see God talking to His people in the Old Testament about love and again in the new testament about love many times.

And you shall love the Lord your God with all your [mind and] heart and with your entire being and with all your might.
Deuteronomy 6:5 (AMP)

And He answering said, "You shall love the Lord your God with all your heart, and with all your soul, and with all your strength, and with all your mind; and your neighbor as yourself."
Luke 10:27 (AMP)

"Teacher, which kind of commandment is great and important (the principal kind) in the Law? [Some commandments are light—which are heavy?]." And He replied to him, "You shall love the Lord your God with all your heart and with

all your soul and with all your mind (intellect). This is the great (most important, principal) and first commandment. And a second is like it: You shall love your neighbor as [you do] yourself. These two commandments sum up and upon them depend all the Law and the Prophets. On these two commandments hang all the law and the prophets." (He was talking about the new commandment to love God and love people as yourself).

Matthew 22:36 (AMP)

God is in us. God is love and we must live a life of love. A lifestyle of love.

I John 4:16, "And so we know and rely on the love God has for us. God is love. Whoever lives in love lives in God, and God in them."

We must not live our lives like the world lives their lives or think like the world thinks. When the world thinks retaliation and payback, but God is telling us that is sin.

"If you love those who love you, what credit is that to you? Even sinners love those who love them. And if you do good to those who are good to you, what credit is that to you? Even sinners do that. And if you lend to those from whom you expect repayment, what credit is that to you? Even sinners lend to sinners, expecting to be repaid in full. But love your enemies, do good to them, and lend to them without expecting to get any-

thing back. Then your reward will be great, and you will be children of the Most High, because He is kind to the ungrateful and wicked. Be merciful, just as your Father is merciful."

Luke 6:32-36 (KJV)

According to the word of God, we are nothing if we do not have love. Wow, that is so important to God that we love. In this scripture of I Corinthians chapter thirteen, it is clear that we should check our motives when we do things to benefit others as well. We do acts of love to be a blessing to others and not for our own glory, but to glorify God.

If I [can] speak in the tongues of men and [even] of angels, but have not love (that reasoning, intentional, spiritual devotion such as is inspired by God's love for and in us), I am only a noisy gong or a clanging cymbal. And if I have prophetic powers (the gift of interpreting the divine will and purpose), and understand all the secret truths and mysteries and possess all knowledge, and if I have [sufficient] faith so that I can remove mountains, but have not love (God's love in me) I am nothing (a useless nobody). Even if I dole out all that I have [to the poor in providing] food, and if I surrender my body to be burned or in order that I may glory, but have not love (God's love in me), I gain nothing.

I Corinthians 13:1-3 (AMP)

He will show mercy to many generations when we love God and keep His commandments. "But showing mercy and steadfast love to a thousand generations of those who love Me and keep My commandments" (Exodus 20:6, KJV). This means no revenge as in Leviticus 19:18, "You shall not take revenge or bear any grudge against the sons of your people, but you shall love your neighbor as yourself. I am the Lord." And again we see in Leviticus 19:34, "But the stranger who dwells with you shall be to you as one born among you; and you shall love him as yourself, for you were strangers in the land of Egypt. I am the Lord your God."

Because the Lord loves us, He is willing to set us free from our bondages. Not only out of Egypt (the world) but our own personal house of bondage, or "issues," we may have to deal with and be free from. But, this freedom comes with a cost and the price is love and surrender of all to Him.

But because the Lord loves you and because He would keep the oath which He had sworn to your fathers, the Lord has brought you out with a mighty hand and redeemed you out of the house of bondage, from the hand of Pharaoh king of Egypt. Know, recognize, and understand therefore that the Lord your God, He is God, the faithful God, Who keeps covenant and steadfast love and mercy with those who love Him and keep His commandments, to a thousand generations, and if you hearken to these precepts and keep and do them, the Lord your God will keep with you the covenant and the steadfast love which He swore to your fathers. And He will love you, bless you, and multiply you; He will also bless the fruit of your body and the fruit of your land, your grain, your new wine, and your oil, the increase of your cattle and the young of your flock in the land which He swore to your fathers to give you.

Deuteronomy 7:8-13 (KJV)

And now, Israel, what does the Lord your God require of you but [reverently] to fear the Lord your God, [that is] to walk in all His ways, and to love Him, and to serve the Lord your God with all your [mind and] heart and with your entire being.

Deuteronomy 10:12, (AMP)

For if you diligently keep all this commandment which I command you to do, to love the Lord your God, to walk in all His ways, and to cleave to Him. Then the Lord will drive out all these nations before you, and you shall dispossess nations greater and mightier than you. Every place upon which the sole of your foot shall tread shall be yours: from the wilderness to Lebanon, and from the River, the river Euphrates, to the western sea [the Mediterranean] your territory shall be. There shall no man be able to stand before you; the Lord your God shall lay the fear and the dread of you upon all the land that you shall tread, as He has said to you. Behold, I set before you this day a blessing and a curse. The blessing if you obey the commandments of the Lord your God which I command you *this day; And the curse if you will not obey the commandments of the Lord your God, but turn aside from the way which I command you this day to go after other gods, which you have not known.*

Deuteronomy 11:22-28 (KJV)

Once we come to God and walk in love and holiness, God will not allow anyone to curse His people, though they may try. We see this when Balak tried to get Balaam have curses sent to God's people. "Nevertheless, the Lord your God would not listen to Balaam, but the Lord your God turned the curse into a blessing to you, because the Lord your God loves you." When the people of God were not in sin they could not be cursed, when they loved God and walked in His ways. However, we see later when they fell in sin with men and women through fornication and mixing with the worldly relationships, they were able to be cursed.

And the Lord your God will circumcise your hearts and the hearts of your descendants, to love the Lord your God with all your [mind and] heart and with all your being, that you may live. If you obey the commandments of the Lord your God which] I command you today, to love the Lord your God, to walk in His ways, and to keep His commandments and His statutes and His ordinances, then you shall live and multiply, and the Lord your God will bless you in the land into which you go to possess.

Deuteronomy 30:6,16 (AMP)

Remember not the sins (the lapses and frailties) of my youth or my transgressions; according to Your mercy and steadfast love remember me, for Your goodness' sake, O Lord. All the paths of the Lord are mercy and steadfast love, even truth and faithfulness are they for those who keep His covenant and His testimonies.

Psalms 25:7, 10 (AMP)

Anything outside of love will cause us to sin and if we continue to sin without repentance there will be iniquity in our hearts. Iniquity, willful and unrepented sin, will also allow sickness in the body.

I will be glad and rejoice in Your mercy and steadfast love, because You have seen my affliction, You have taken note of my life's distresses, And You have not given me into the hand of the enemy; You have set my feet in a broad place. Have mercy and be gracious unto me, O Lord, for I am in trouble; with grief my eye is weakened, also my inner self and my body. For my life is spent with sorrow and my years with sighing; my strength has failed because of my iniquity, and even my bones have wasted away. O love the Lord, all you His saints! The

Lord preserves the faithful, and plentifully pays back him who deals haughtily.

Psalms 31:7-10:23 (KJV)

How precious is Your steadfast love, O God! The children of men take refuge and put their trust under the shadow of Your wings. For in You, O Lord, do I hope; You will answer, O Lord my God. For I do confess my guilt and iniquity; I am filled with sorrow for my sin. But my enemies are vigorous and strong, and those who hate me wrongfully are multiplied. They also that render evil for good are adversaries to me, because I follow the thing that is good. Forsake me not, O Lord; O my God, be not far from me. Make haste to help me, O Lord, my Salvation.

Psalm 36:7,15,19-22 (KJV)

God will deliver us from the enemy when we choose to love. "*Because* He has set His love upon Me, therefore will I deliver him; I will set him on high, because he knows *and* understands My name [has a personal knowledge of My mercy, *love*, and kindness—trusts and relies on Me, knowing I will never forsake him, no, never]" (Psalms 91:14, AMP). And the Lord will, "preserve all those who love Him" (Psalms 145:20, AMP).

For I will delight myself in Your commandments, which I love. My hands also will I lift up [in fervent supplication] to Your commandments, which I love, and I will meditate on Your statutes. Let, I pray You, Your merciful kindness and steadfast love be for my comfort, according to Your promise to Your servant. Look upon me, be merciful unto me, and show me favor, as is Your way to those who love Your name. Hear my voice according to Your steadfast love; O Lord, quicken me and give me life according to Your [righteous] decrees. Consider how I love Your precepts; revive me and give life to me, O Lord, according to Your loving-kindness! Great peace have they who love Your law; nothing shall offend them or make them stumble.

Psalms 119:47-48,132,149,159,165 (AMP)

The way of the wicked is an abomination, extremely disgusting and shamefully vile to the Lord, but He loves him who pursues righteousness (moral and spiritual rectitude in every area and relation).

Proverbs 15:9 (AMP)

By mercy and love, truth and fidelity [to God and man—not by sacrificial offerings], iniquity is purged out of the heart, and by the reverent, worshipful fear of the Lord men depart from and avoid evil. Right and just lips are the delight of a king, and he loves him who speaks what is right.

Proverbs 16:6,13 (AMP)

You have heard that it was said, 'You shall love your neighbor and hate your enemy;' But I tell you, Love your enemies and pray for those who persecute you, To show that you are the children of your Father Who is in heaven; for He makes His sun rise on the wicked and on the good, and makes the rain fall upon the upright and the wrongdoers [alike]. For if you love those who love you, what reward can you have? Do not even the tax collectors do that? And if you greet only your brethren, what more than others are you doing? Do not even the Gentiles (the heathen) do that? You, therefore, must be perfect [growing into complete maturity of godliness in mind and character, having reached the proper height of virtue and integrity], as your heavenly Father is perfect.

Matthew 5:43-48 (AMP)

But I say to you who are listening now to Me: [in order to heed, make it a practice to] love your enemies, treat well (do good to, act nobly toward) those who detest you and pursue you with hatred, If you [merely] love those who love you, what quality of credit and thanks is that to you? For even the [very] sinners love their lovers (those who love them).

Luke 6:27,32,35 (AMP)

The [basis of the] judgment (indictment, the test by which men are judged, the ground for the sentence) lies in this: The Light has come into the world, and people have loved the darkness rather than and more than the Light, for their works (deeds) were evil.

John 3:19 (AMP)

When people see us, they should be able to see the love of God in us. "*But I know you and recognize and understand that you have not the love of God in you.*

John 5:42 (AMP)

They will know that we are of God by our love.

By this shall all men know that ye are my disciples, if ye have love one to another.

John 13:35 (KJV)

If you [really] love Me, you will keep (obey) My commands. The person who has My commands and keeps them is the one who [really] loves Me; and whoever [really] loves Me will be loved by My Father, and I [too] will love him and will show (reveal, manifest) Myself to him. [I will let Myself be clearly seen by him and make Myself real to him.]. Jesus answered, If a person [really] loves Me, he will keep My word [obey My teaching]; and My Father will love him, and We will come to him and make Our home (abode, special dwelling place) with him. Anyone who does not [really] love Me does not observe and obey My teaching. And the teaching which you hear and heed is not Mine, but [comes] from the Father Who sent

Me. You heard Me tell you, I am going away and I am coming [back] to you. If you [really] loved Me, you would have been glad, because I am going to the Father; for the Father is greater and mightier than I am.

John 14:15, 21,23,24,28 (AMP)

We already have the love of God in us. "Such hope never disappoints or deludes or shames us, for God's love has been poured out in our hearts through the Holy Spirit Who has been given to us" (Romans 5:5, AMP). "[Let your] *love* be sincere (a real thing); hate what is evil [loathe all ungodliness, turn in horror from wickedness], but hold fast to that which is good. *Love* one another with brotherly affection [as members of one family], giving precedence *and* showing honor to one another" (Romans 12:9-10, AMP). It is written in the holy Word of God that we are nothing without love.

If I [can] speak in the tongues of men and [even] of angels, but have not love (that reasoning, intentional, spiritual devotion such as is inspired by God's love for and in us), I am only a noisy gong or a clanging cymbal. And if I have prophetic powers (the gift of interpreting the divine will and purpose), and understand all the secret truths and mysteries and possess all knowledge, and if I have [sufficient] faith so that I can remove mountains, but have not love (God's love in me) I am nothing (a useless nobody). Even if I dole out all that I have [to the poor in providing] food, and if I surrender my body to be burned or in order that I may glory, but have not love (God's love in me), I gain nothing. Love endures long and is patient and kind; love never is envious nor boils over with jealousy, is not boastful or vainglorious, does not display itself haughtily. It is not conceited (arrogant and inflated with pride); it is not rude (unmannerly) and does not act unbecomingly. Love (God's love in us) does not insist on its own rights or its own way, for it is not self-seeking; it is not touchy or fretful or resentful; it takes no account of the evil done to it [it pays no attention to a suffered wrong]. Love bears up under anything and everything that comes, is ever ready to believe the best of every person, its hopes are fadeless under all circumstances, and it endures everything [without weakening]. Love never fails [never fades out or becomes obsolete or comes to an end]. As for prophecy (the gift of interpreting the divine will and purpose), it will be fulfilled and pass away; as for tongues, they will be destroyed and cease; as for knowledge, it will pass away [it will lose its value and be superseded by truth]. And so faith, hope, love abide [faith—conviction and belief respecting man's relation to God and divine things; hope—joyful and confident expectation of eternal salvation; love—true affection for God and man, growing out of God's love for and in us], these three; but the greatest of these is love.

I Corinthians 13:1-13 (AMP)

We are to actually pursue, make an effort, to cultivate the love of God that has been poured into our hearts. "Eagerly pursue and seek to acquire [this] love [make it your aim, your great quest]; and earnestly desire and cultivate the spiritual endowments (gifts), especially that you may prophesy (interpret the divine will and purpose in inspired preaching and teaching) (I Corinthians 14:1, AMP).

Everything we do, must be done in love if we are to be pleasing to God. If we walk in His ways and we walk in love, always. This is not always easy to do with those that hurt you, especially if they are currently causing you trouble and are having to deal with them in the present.

Let everything you do be done in love (true love to God and man as inspired by God's love for us). If anyone does not love the Lord [does not have a friendly affection for Him and is not kindly disposed toward Him], he shall be accursed! Our Lord will come! (Maranatha!). My love (that true love growing out of sincere devotion to God) be with you all in Christ Jesus.
I Corinthians 16:14, 22,24 (AMP)

One of the ways we show love is by our giving to help others with our finances and our resources.

> *Now as you abound and excel and are at the front in everything—in faith, in expressing yourselves, in knowledge, in all zeal, and in your love for us [see to it that you come to the front now and] abound and excel in this gracious work [of almsgiving] also. I give this not as an order [to dictate to you], but to prove, by [pointing out] the zeal of others, the sincerity of your [own] love also. Show to these men, therefore, in the sight of the churches, the reality and plain truth of your love (your affection, goodwill, and benevolence) and what [good reasons] I had for boasting about and being proud of you.*
>
> II Corinthians 8:7 (AMP)

> *Let each one [give] as he has made up his own mind and purposed in his heart, not reluctantly or sorrowfully or under compulsion, for God loves (He takes pleasure in, prizes above other things, and is unwilling to abandon or to do without) a cheerful (joyous, "prompt to do it") giver [whose heart is in his giving].*
>
> II Corinthians 9:7 (AMP)

If we live in love, and have a lifestyle of love, we know that God will be with us. He is the promoter of peace and we should not be in conflict, anger, bitterness against others. He is with us as we love others.

Finally, brethren, farewell (rejoice)! Be strengthened (perfected, completed, made what you ought to be); be encour-

aged and consoled and comforted; be of the same [agreeable] mind one with another; live in peace, and [then] the God of love [Who is the Source of affection, goodwill, love, and benevolence toward men] and the Author and Promoter of peace will be with you. The grace (favor and spiritual blessing) of the Lord Jesus Christ and the love of God and the presence and fellowship (the communion and sharing together, and participation) in the Holy Spirit be with you all. Amen, so be it.
II Corinthians 13:11,14 (AMP)

We are to live our life not our will be done, but according to how God desires us to live.

I have been crucified with Christ [in Him I have shared His crucifixion]; it is no longer I who live, but Christ (the Messiah) lives in me; and the life I now live in the body I live by faith in (by adherence to and reliance on and complete trust in) the Son of God, Who loved me and gave Himself up for me.
Galatians 2:20 (AMP)

Even our faith works by love. "For [if we are] in Christ Jesus, neither circumcision nor uncircumcision counts for anything, but only faith activated and energized and expressed and working through love" (Galatians 5:6, AMP). For in Jesus Christ, neither circumcision availeth anything, nor uncircumcision; but faith which worketh by love" (Galatians 5:6, KJV).

We have the Holy Spirt in us and His love. This love should be growing, and we should be maturing in love. Galatians 5:22 says, "But the fruit of the [Holy] Spirit [the work which His presence within accomplishes] is *love*, joy (gladness), peace, patience (an even temper, forbearance), kindness, goodness (benevolence), faithfulness." This love is so important to God, He said we are to be above reproach, before Him in love.

Even as [in His love] He chose us [actually picked us out for Himself as His own] in Christ before the foundation of the world, that we should be holy (consecrated and set apart for Him) and blameless in His sight, even above reproach, before Him in love. For He foreordained us (destined us, planned in love for us) to be adopted (revealed) as His own children through Jesus Christ, in accordance with the purpose of His will [because it pleased Him and was His kind intent].

Ephesians 1:4-5 (AMP)

We should love others so well with the real love of God that others will hear about the great love that the body of Christ has for people as in Ephesians 1:15, "Wherefore I also, after I heard of your faith in the Lord Jesus, and love unto all the saints." Our love should be on display, so that others may see the love of Christ in us.

God is merciful and loves us with "intense love" (Ephesians 2:4). We are to be rooted and grounded in this love.

May Christ through your faith [actually] dwell (settle down, abide, make His permanent home) in your hearts! May you be rooted deep in love and founded securely on love. That you may have the power and be strong to apprehend and grasp with all the saints [God's devoted people, the experience of that love] what is the breadth and length and height and depth [of it]; [That you may really come] to know [practically, through experience for yourselves] the love of Christ, which far surpasses mere knowledge [without experience]; that you may be filled [through all your being] unto all the fullness of God [may have the richest measure of the divine Presence, and become a body wholly filled and flooded with God Himself]!
Ephesians 3:17-19 (AMP)

Living as becomes you] with complete lowliness of mind (humility) and meekness (unselfishness, gentleness, mildness), with patience, bearing with one another and making allowances because you love one another.
Ephesians 4:2 (AMP)

Rather, let our lives lovingly express truth [in all things, speaking truly, dealing truly, living truly]. Enfolded in love, let us grow up in every way and in all things into Him Who is the Head, [even] Christ (the Messiah, the Anointed One). For because of Him the whole body (the church, in all its various parts), closely joined and firmly knit together by the joints and ligaments with which it is supplied, when each part [with power adapted to its need] is working properly [in all its functions], grows to full maturity, building itself up in love.

Ephesians 4:15 (AMP)

[The Father] has delivered and drawn us to Himself out of the control and the dominion of darkness and has transferred us into the kingdom of the Son of His love.

Colossians 1:13 (AMP)

Above everything, above the spiritual gifts, above everything we are to desire and first put on love. "And above all these [put on] love and enfold yourselves with the bond of perfectness [which binds everything together completely in ideal harmony]" (Colossians 3:14, AMP). We are to excel in this love more and more. We have the love of God in us, but we must stir it up and display it.

But concerning brotherly love [for all other Christians], you have no need to have anyone write you, for you yourselves have been [personally] taught by God to love one another. And indeed, you already are [extending and displaying your love] to all the brethren throughout Macedonia. But we beseech and earnestly exhort you, brethren, that you excel [in this matter] more and more.

1 Thessalonians 4:9-10 (AMP)

And let us consider and give attentive, continuous care to watching over one another, studying how we may stir up (stimulate and incite) to love and helpful deeds and noble activities.

Hebrews 10:24 (AMP)

Let love for your fellow believers continue and be a fixed practice with you [never let it fail]. Let your character or moral disposition be free from love of money [including greed, avarice, lust, and craving for earthly possessions] and be satisfied with your present [circumstances and with what you have]; for He [God] Himself has said, I will not in any way fail you nor give you up nor leave you without support. [I will] not, [I will] not, [I will] not in any degree leave you helpless nor forsake nor let [you] down (relax My hold on you)! [Assuredly not!].

Hebrews 13:1,5 (AMP)

Since by your obedience to the Truth through the [Holy] Spirit you have purified your hearts for the sincere affection of the brethren, [see that you] love one another fervently from a pure heart.

I Peter 1:22 (AMP)

Show respect for all men [treat them honorably]. Love the brotherhood (the Christian fraternity of which Christ is the Head). Reverence God. Honor the Emperor.

I Peter 2:17 (AMP)

Above all things have intense and unfailing love for one another, for love covers a multitude of sins [forgives and disregards the offenses of others]. Practice hospitality to one another (those of the household of faith). [Be hospitable, be a lover of strangers, with brotherly affection for the unknown guests, the foreigners, the poor, and all others who come your way who are of Christ's body.] And [in each instance] do it ungrudgingly (cordially and graciously, without complaining but as representing Him).

1 Peter 4:8-9 (AMP)

See what [an incredible] quality of love the Father has given (shown, bestowed on) us, that we should [be permitted to] be named and called and counted the children of God! And so we are! The reason that the world does not know (recognize, acknowledge) us is that it does not know (recognize, acknowledge) Him. By this it is made clear who take their nature from God and are His children and who take their nature from the devil and are his children: no one who does not practice righteousness [who does not conform to God's will in purpose, thought, and action] is of God; neither is anyone who does not love his brother (his fellow believer in Christ). For this is the message (the announcement) which you have heard from the first, that we should love one another. We know that we have passed over out of death into Life by the fact that we love the brethren (our fellow Christians). He who does not love abides (remains, is held and kept continually) in [spiritual] death.

By this we come to know (progressively to recognize, to perceive, to understand) the [essential] love: that He laid down His [own] life for us; and we ought to lay [our] lives down for [those who are our] brothers [in Him]. But if anyone has this world's goods (resources for sustaining life) and sees his brother and fellow believer in need, yet closes his heart of compassion against him, how can the love of God live and remain in him? Little children let us not love [merely] in theory or in speech but in deed and in truth (in practice and in sincerity). And this is His order (His command, His injunction): that we should believe in (put our faith and trust in and adhere to and rely on) the name of His Son Jesus Christ (the Messiah), and that we should love one another, just as He has commanded us.

1 John 3:1, 10, 11, 14,16-18,23 (AMP)

Beloved, let us love one another, for love is (springs) from God; and he who loves [his fellowmen] is begotten (born) of God and is coming [progressively] to know and understand God [to perceive and recognize and get a better and clearer knowledge of Him]. He who does not love has not become acquainted with God [does not and never did know Him], for God is love. In this the love of God was made manifest (displayed) where we are concerned: in that God sent His Son, the only begotten or unique [Son], into the world so that we might live through Him. In this is love: not that we loved God, but that He loved us and sent His Son to be the propitiation (the atoning sacrifice) for our sins. Beloved, if God loved us so [very much], we also ought to love one another. No man has at any time [yet] seen God. But if we love one another, God abides (lives and remains) in us and His love (that love which is essentially His) is brought to completion (to its full maturity, runs its full course, is perfected) in us! And we know (understand, recognize, are conscious of, by observation and by experience) and believe (adhere to and put faith in and rely on) the love God cherishes for us. God is love, and he who dwells and continues in love dwells and continues in God, and God dwells and continues in him. In this [union and communion with Him] love is brought to completion and attains perfection with us, that we may have confidence for the day of judgment [with assurance and boldness to face Him], because as He is, so are we in this world. There is no fear in love [dread does not exist], but full-grown (complete, perfect) love turns fear out of doors and expels every trace of terror! For fear brings with it the thought of punishment, and [so] he who is afraid has not reached the full maturity of love [is not yet grown into love's complete perfection]. We love Him, because He first loved us. If anyone says, 'I love God,' and hates (detests, abominates) his brother [in Christ], he is a liar; for he who does not love his brother, whom he has seen, cannot love God, Whom he has not seen. And this command (charge, order, injunction) we have from Him: that he who loves God shall love his brother [believer] also.

1 John 4:7-21 (AMP)

And now I beg you, lady (Cyria), not as if I were issuing a new charge (injunction or command), but [simply recalling to your mind] the one we have had from the beginning, that we love one another. And what this love consists in is this: that we live and walk in accordance with and guided by His commandments (His orders, ordinances, precepts, teaching). This is the commandment, as you have heard from the beginning, that you continue to walk in love [guided by it and following it].

2 John 1:5-6 (AMP)

The first step to deliverance and freedom is to come to God. For those that have turned back to the ways of the world and darkness, and away from the Kingdom of Light and God, who is love, should turn quickly back to God and repent. "But I have this [one charge to make] against you: that you have left (abandoned) the *love* that you had at first [you have deserted Me, your first *love*]" (Revelation 2:4, AMP).

Once we repent and ask God to forgive us of our sins, His powerful blood of Jesus will wash us clean from all of our sins. "The [basis of the] judgment (indictment, the test by which men are judged, the ground for the sentence) lies in this: the Light has come into the world, and people have loved the darkness rather than and more than the Light, for their works (deeds) were evil" (John 3:19, AMP).

And from Jesus Christ the faithful and trustworthy witness, the Firstborn of the dead [first to be brought back to life] and the Prince (ruler) of the kings of the Earth. To Him

Whoever loves us and has once [for all] loosed and freed us from our sins by His own Blood.

Revelation 1:5 (AMP)

CHAPTER EIGHTEEN

How to Be Delivered

We must have compassion for those who require deliverance from demons. God makes it easy for us to live a life of freedom if we follow His instructions in His love letter to us, His Holy Word. Although Scriptures contains much about love, it is also filled with warnings and direction for our lives.

God has given us authority and power over the enemy. You must recognize the authority that has been delegated to you in the name of Jesus. "In My name, they will cast out demons." But we must be a follower of Christ, imitators of our Father. What we see Him do in the Word, we should do ourselves.

And these signs shall follow those who believe: In My name they will cast out demons; they will speak with new tongues.
Mark 16:17 (AMP)

Here Christ shows two manifestations of supernatural power which are to confirm the testimony of Cristian believers. We do not hear very much about casting out demons in the church today; however, it is the first sign that will follow believers. There needs to be understanding and discernment practiced in the church.

We have the power of the Holy Spirit. Jesus said, "If I cast out demons by the Spirit of God, surely the kingdom of God has come upon you" (Matthew 12:28, AMP). Likewise, He attributed to the anointing of the Holy Spirit His ability to "proclaim liberty [or deliverance] to the captives ... to set at liberty those who are oppressed" (Isaiah 6:1, AMP). We have redemption through the blood of Jesus.

We know through this study that God requires us to live a life of love, be love, do acts of kindness and love. Love God, love everyone, and love our self. If we miss it in some area of our love walk and continually sin, and have tried to gain freedom, and after fasting, praying, but still continue with the same spiritual issue you probably need deliverance. You may be under the influence or power of demons.

Another means by which the presence or activity of demons may be detected is the supernatural manifestation of the Holy Spirit called, "discerning of spirits" as in I Corinthians chapter twelve and verse ten. Discernment of this kind needs to be cultivated by regular exercise. "Who are of full age [maturity], that is, those who by reason of use have their senses exorcised to discern both good and evil" (Hebrews 5:14, AMP).

First the person needs to recognize that he has a spiritual problem and wants to be free from it. There are some people that want to be free from the torment caused by the demons, but do not want to give up the sin in their lives that is causing the open door: for example, fornication, adultery, gossiping, watching horror movies, bitterness, resentment, gambling addictions, pornography, etc.

There are some people that are living in sin and believe it is okay. These types of people will not receive their complete deliverance until they are willing to give up the sin. In praying for someone like this, we should pray that they will come to know the truth and that the Holy Spirit will convict them, and they will truly repent and serve the Lord with all their heart.

If someone feels they are oppressed by a demonic spirit, after they recognize their bondage, they must humble themselves before God, then submit to God (be obedient to His Word). Ask the Holy Spirit to show them where there is an open door, where is there any sin in their life that they may not recognize that they have. It may be something like strife and not realizing it is sin and have never dealt with it before.

But whether it is unforgiveness, pride, lust, involvement with the occult, anger, perversion, or any other sins, you must be honest about it, acknowledge it, and confess it. "Confess your trespasses one to another" (James 5:16, KJV).

You must renounce the sin. "He who covers his transgressions will not prosper but, whoever confesses and forsakes his sins will have mercy" (Proverbs 28:13, KJV). "Let the wicked forsake his way, and the unrighteous man his thoughts; let him return to the Lord, and He will have mercy on him; and to our God, for He will abundantly pardon" (Isaiah 55:7, KJV). The sinner must not only forsake "his way" (his outward acts), but also "his thoughts" (any inward sinful leanings or desires, even though these are not expressed in outward acts). "Forsaking must come before "mercy" and "pardon."

"The one who desires forgiveness from God must first forgive his fellow men. Resentment and an unforgiving spirit are two of the commonest hinderances to deliverance. In Hebrews 12:15 we are warned against "any root of bitterness." Wherever bitterness has poisoned the heart, it must be totally removed, so that not even a root is left" (Prince, *Expelling Demons*, 16).

There is special significance in the order of words in the Lord's Prayer in Matthew 6:9-13. First, "Forgive us our debts [or trespasses], as we forgive our debtors [or those who trespass against us]." That is to say, our forgiveness from God is in proportion to our forgiveness of our fellow men. Then, "Deliver us from the evil one." That is to say, forgiveness must come before deliverance. Without forgiveness, we have no right to deliverance.

After forgiving everyone who has hurt you, repent and ask God to forgive you for your sin. Then "Whosoever calls on the name of the Lord shall be saved [or delivered]" (Joel 2:32). By the authority and in the name of Jesus, command the evil spirit to leave you, or the person if you are ministering to someone.

It is important to realize that deliverance is normally a process. This process may be brief or long and drawn out, it may be intense and dramatic, or it may be quiet and scarcely perceptible. Unless the demon actually comes out, there has been no deliverance.

If we confess our sin, ask God to forgive us, renounce it, forgive everyone, decide and determine to love God, love people and love our self; after that, the enemy has no right or legal authority in our life (see chapter on legal rights of the enemy). Then we can command the demon spirit to "go in the name of Jesus the Christ of Nazareth."

However, although we can command the demon to leave without having the person repent, demons have a legal right to stay because the person is living a lifestyle of sin; even though they may leave temporarily they can and will try to return.

As for the believer that truly repents, and has a sincere desire to serve the Lord, and walk in His ways of love and mercy and is completely delivered, the demon will try to return but will have no right into his life again. This is where the believer must remain submitted to God and His Word and the very second the demon tries to put wrong thoughts in your mind to do the sin again, or negative thoughts against someone who wronged you, thoughts of resentment, unloving thoughts, immediately, the very second the thought comes, cast down the thoughts "in the name of Jesus" and command it to "go." Do not entertain the wrong thoughts for even one second. You will remain free in Christ.

Where the spirit of the Lord is there is liberty. "Now the Lord is the Spirit, and where the Spirit of the Lord is, there is liberty (emancipation from bondage, freedom)" (2 Corinthians 3:17, AMP). "It is the anointing that breaks the yoke" (Isaiah 10:27, KJV). You that are true believers in Jesus, that allow Him to be the Lord over every area of your life, you have the authority and the power to drive out evil spirits that would try to come against you. It is the will of God for you to be free from any demonic oppression, and that you in turn set the captives free in the name of Jesus, and it is a sign that follows believers.

> "The church of Jesus Christ is being confronted by the same manifest opposition of demon power that confronted the church of the New Testament. In these circumstances, the church must again explore the resources of authority and power made available to her through the truth of Scripture, the anointing of the Holy Spirit, and the name and the blood of the Lord Jesus Christ"
> (Prince, *Expelling Demons*, 20).

When we pray to God we pray with our heart in true repentance and sincerity. This is a sample of a simple yet powerful prayer model for deliverance. However, remember from this teaching and the scriptures that have been given to you concerning the number one block to receiving deliverance and healing is when you do not forgive those that have wronged you. Before praying, forgive everyone and release those who have sinned against you, so you may be forgiven and released by God the Father.

Simple sample prayer to help you:

I forgive all persons, living or dead, who have injured me or spoken evil toward me. I forgive them, so I also may be forgiven. I forgive _____ and I release him/her in the name of Jesus. (There may be more than one person or many but you must forgive every person, so there is no open door to the enemy).

Heavenly Father, my God, I come to you in the name of your son Jesus the Christ of Nazereth. I recognize I have participated with the sin of (_____) in my life and I take responsibility for participating with these sinful acts and thoughts of (____) in my life. I confess my sin. In the name of Jesus, I repent to You and ask You to forgive me for allowing the sin of (_____) to manifest through me. By faith, and in the name of Jesus, I now receive Your forgiveness, Heavenly Father and ask to be released from the power of this sin over my life.

I renounce (the sin of _____) and everything you stand for in my life. I will no longer serve you. I take a stand against you and everything you represent. You will no longer rule over my life and no spirit will rule over my life but the Spirit of the living God.

Sin (spirit of_____), I have repented to my Father in heaven for serving you and allowing you to manifest through me. I speak to the strongman that has been trying to control my life and any spirit operating with him. You must leave me now and in the mighty name of Jesus go from me now!

If You Are Doing Ministry for Someone:

After the person that needs deliverance says a similar prayer to the one above, then pray for that person and say:

Sin (Spirit of _____), you heard their confession and declaration. You have to obey them in the name of Jesus. And by the authority and in the name of Jesus the Christ of Nazareth Spirit of (_____), go from this person in the name of Jesus.

You do not have to scream and yell at the demons when you command them to go, that does not impress nor scare them off to leave the person. Speak with a holy boldness with authority and in the name of Jesus the Christ of Nazareth. Use the authority that Jesus already gave you over all the power of the enemy.

As long as the person has no legal right for the enemy (demon) to stay they will have to flee out. "Submit to God, resist the devil, and he will flee" (James 4:7, KJV). Submitting to God means that you are obedient to His Word in every area of your life.

For example, the area of sexual relations outside of marriage will leave an open door for the enemy in your life. About fifteen years ago, we were ministering deliverance to a young handsome man who had many demons. He went to different nations seeking how to be free from the demons that were tormenting him.

Unfortunately for him, not knowing Jesus as his Lord, savior, and deliverer and not knowing how to gain his freedom he was seeking out witch doctors and anyone for help and of course his condition only got worse. Obviously, from a Biblical perspective, we know that visiting witch doctors is a huge open door to the demonic in someone's life.

This young man had been involved in satanic blood covenants and would seek out and sleep with different women to intentionally transfer demonic spirits, while the women were unaware of his intentions. God said that when two come together in intimate relations the two then become one, that is also an open door to the demonic spirits that operate in the other person's life can come into your life if you are in sexual relations with the person.

How to Pray a Prayer for Curses in Your Life:

Lord Jesus Christ, I believe that You are the Son of God and the only way to God. That You died on the cross for my sins and rose again from the dead. That on the cross You were made sin with my sinfulness that I might be made righteous with Your righteousness. And also, that You were made a curse with any curse that might come upon me. Now, Lord, I come to You for deliverance from any such curse. I repent of any sins that have caused it to come, whether by me or by my ancestors. I receive Your forgiveness. I take my stand now against the devil and in the name of Jesus, I resist him. I refuse to submit any longer to him. In the name of Jesus, I now release myself from any curse over my life. Because of what Jesus did for me, in His name I release myself and I receive the release now by faith with thankfulness. Lord, I thank You now. I praise You now. I believe You're faithful. I believe You are doing what I've asked You to do. I thank You and praise You, I commit my life to You—that from now on, Your blessing may rest upon me. Thank You, Lord Jesus. Thank You!

CHAPTER NINETEEN

How to Keep Your Deliverance

God wants you to live a life of freedom. Now that the power of the devil that has been working in your life is broken and you are released, you must appropriate your freedom, day by day.

A Brief Summary of Steps Taken to Receive Deliverance

Recognize:

At this point, you have already recognized you had a problem and what it was by the conviction (not condemnation) of the Holy Spirit. You don't say, "That is just the way I am." You have taken responsibility.

"But we all, with open face beholding as in a glass (mirror) the glory of the Lord, are changed into the same image from glory to glory, even as by the Spirit of the Lord" (2 Corinthians 3:18, AMP). You must let God change you.

You realized that you have had sin in your life. "For I acknowledge my transgressions: and my sin is ever before me. Against thee, thee only have I sinned, and done this evil in thy sight: that thou mightest be justified when thou speakest and be clear when thou judges" (Psalm 51:3-4, KJV).

Repent:

You have repented to God for participating in the sin that you have recognized. "Repent ye therefore, and be converted, that your sins may be blotted out, when the times of refreshing shall come from the presence of the Lord" (Acts 3:19, KJV).

"Therefore, I will judge you, O house of Israel, everyone according to his ways, saith the Lord God. Repent, and turn yourselves from all your transgressions; so iniquity shall not be your ruin" (Ezekiel 18:30, KJV).

"If we confess our sins, He is faithful and just to forgive us our sins, and to cleanse us from all unrighteousness" (I John 1:9, KJV).

"Remember therefor from whence thou are fallen, and repent, and do the first works; or else I will come unto thee quickly, and will remove they candlestick out of his place, except thou repent" (Revelation 2:5, KJV).

God will give you space to repent but if you do not repent His word says, "And I gave her space to repent of her fornication; and she repented not. Behold, I will cast her into a bed, and them that commit adultery with her into great tribulation, except they repent of their deeds" (Revelation 2:21-22, KJV).

"Remember therefore how thou hast received and heard, and hold fast, and repent. If therefore thou shalt not watch, I will come on thee as a thief, and thou shalt not know what hour I will come upon thee" (Revelation 3:3, KJV).

Renounce:

When you repent you must truly mean it in your heart. You may have remorse but do not change on the inside. To repent means to "turn away from." God told us to turn away from sin or it would be our ruin.

"Ye cannot drink the cup of the Lord, and the cup of devils: Ye cannot be partakers of the Lord's table, and of the table of devils. Do we provoke the Lord to jealousy? Are we stronger than He?" (I Corinthians 10:21-22, KJV).

Get away from evil - renounce it as fast as you can. Separate yourself from evil. Love your neighbor, but not the evil he does. Learn to separate yourself and others from their sin.

Remove:

Remove the sin and tell it to go and that it cannot stay. "Cast away from you all your transgressions, whereby ye have transgressed; and make you a new heart and a new spirit: for why will you die, O house of Israel?" (Ezekiel 18:3, KJV).

Resist:

We know from the scriptures we do have to resist the devil in order for him to flee from us. "Submit yourselves to God. Resist the devil and he will flee from you" (James 4:7, KJV). The first part of this scripture is submitting to God first, then you will have power over your enemies, not before. Also, "obedience is better than sacrifice, for rebellion is as the sin of witchcraft and stubbornness is as idolatry" (I Samuel 15:22-23, KJV). We must submit to the will of God, the Word of God, and not be stubborn.

Once you have evicted (driven out) evil spirits, God tells us in His Word that they will try to come back to you, but you must resist. "When the unclean spirit is gone out of a man, he walks through dry places, seeking rest; and finding none, he saith, I will return unto my house whence I came out" (Luke 11:24, KJV).

Rejoice:

Give all the thanks and glory to God for your blessing of freedom. Thank Him for His love, His mercy, His grace, praise Him because He alone is worthy to be praised. He is the deliverer.

Restore:

Now that you know how to be delivered, help others to gain their freedom, and break the chains of iniquity and sin. Help to restore others by sharing the truth and the delivering power of the love of the God. And bear one another's burdens.

"But this is a people robbed and spoiled; they are all of them snared in holes, and they are hid in prison houses: they are for a prey and none delivereth; for a spoil, and none saith, Restore" (Isaiah 42:22, KJV).

"Restore unto me the joy of Thy salvation; and uphold me with thy free spirit. Then will I teach transgressors thy ways; and sinners shall be converted unto thee" (Psalm 51:12-13, KJV).

"Brethren, if a man be overtaken in a fault, ye which are spiritual, restore such a one in the spirit of meekness; considering thyself, lest thou also be tempted. Bear ye one another's burdens, and so fulfill the law of Christ. For if a man think himself to be something, when he is nothing, he deceiveth himself" (Galatians 6:1-3, KJV).

How To Maintain Your Freedom

As discussed earlier, we know from the scriptures that the enemy will try to come back. Now what do you do? You will need to know how to deal with them. You will have to make choices. Well, you do not continue reacting the same way as in times past when you were in bondage.

You must renew your mind with the word of God, have your thoughts, attitudes and have a lifestyle according to the word of God. Put away all sin from you. Break any ungodly habits.

"And be renewed in the spirit of your mind" (Ephesians 4:23, KJV). Deliverance is not always a quick fix. Yes, the enemy has fled; however, you still must replace wrong thoughts, behaviors, and habits with godly ones. As you do this, you will create new patterns of righteous behavior.

However, when these entities try to come back to you through thoughts you have to take the authority that God has given you and the powerful name of Jesus and command them to go and to leave you now in the name of Jesus. You, not anyone else, have to tell them to, "Go, in the name of Jesus the Christ of Nazareth" You are the one that knows your own thoughts and when the enemy is trying to harass you with thoughts of fear, loneliness, rejection, resentment, lust, timidity, failure; and the list goes on and on how he tries to operate in the area of the thoughts and minds of even God's people.

There are many people that are walking around that have a smile on the outside but on the inside are dying, having thoughts of suicide and death, and previous to those thoughts were hopelessness, sadness and despair. They are being held captive by an unseen enemy because they don't understand how he operates or how to walk in the freedom that Jesus already purchased for them. They don't understand they have all power and authority over the enemy. To walk in this freedom, one must take every thought captive to the obedience of Christ.

Continue to Walk in Victory

1. When the enemy tries to come back, the word says he will try, if he finds the house empty, he can come in and bring other spirits with him. You must keep your house filled with the Word of God. Strengthen your relationship with the God through not only reading His Word but also times of prayer, talking to God and praise and worship.

That He might sanctify and cleanse it with the washing of water by the Word.
Ephesians 5:26 (KJV)

2. Protect your mind and your thought life. The mind really is the battlefield where our enemy tries to operate the most in the lives of the believer. Discern good from evil. The battle starts in your mind.

For though we walk in the flesh, we do not war after the flesh: (For the weapons of our warfare are not carnal, but mighty through God to the pulling down strong holds;). Casting down imaginations, and every high thing that exalts itself against the knowledge of God, and bringing into captivity every thought to the obedience of Christ: And having in a readiness to revenge all disobedience, when your obedience is fulfilled.
2 Corinthians 10:4-6 (AMP)

Finally, brethren, whatsoever things are true, whatsoever things are honest, whatsoever things are just, whatsoever things are pure, whatsoever things are lovely, whatsoever things are of a good report; if there be any virtue, and if there be any praise, think on these things.
Philippians 4:8 (KJV)

3. Stay away from people that would entice you to sin or any ungodly lifestyle. You may have to reevaluate some of your old relationships. Fellowship with believers that live according to the Word of God.

And they continued steadfastly in the apostles' doctrine and fellowship, and in breaking of bread, and in prayers.
Acts 2:42 (KJV)

4. Forgive. Let go of past failures and traumas. Keep your mind on God.

"...this one thing I do, forgetting those things which are behind, and reaching forth unto those things which are before."
Philippians 3:13 (KJV)

Keep your heart with all diligence; for out of it are the issues of life.
Proverbs 4:23 (KJV)

For we walk by faith, not by sight.
2 Corinthians 5:7 (KJV)

And the tongue is a fire, a world of iniquity: so is the tongue among our members, that it defileth the whole body, and setteth on fire the course of nature; and it is set on fire of hell... But the tongue can no man tame; it is an unruly evil, full of deadly poison.
James 3:6,8 (KJV)

He that walks righteously and speaks uprightly; he that despiseth the gain of oppressions, that shaketh his hands from holding of bribes, that stops his ears from hearing of blood and shutter his eyes from seeing evil; he shall dwell on high....
Isaiah 33:15-16 (KJV)

Stand fast therefore in the liberty wherewith Christ hath made us free and be not entangled again with the yoke of bondage.

Galatians 5:1 (KJV)

SANCTIFICATION:

Sanctification for healing and deliverance is the dimension not being taught much today in the church. As we study and gain knowledge of the Word of God we will not perish for a lack of knowledge. The Holy Spirit can convict us and work through us if we allow Him. We need to listen to God obey His Word. Live a holy lifestyle.

When asked to pray for you if you are not living according to His Word, we should not condone your sin. We cannot ask Him to dishonor His Word and condone your sin. We must be honest and transparent. God knows everything, even the secret thoughts of your heart.

We are to confess our sins, renounce our sins, then God said that we would be healed in James 5:16. "Confess your faults one to another, and pray one for another, that ye may be healed. The effectual fervent prayer of a righteous man availeth much."

Why is it so important to be transparent and confess our sins to God? Because Proverbs 28:13 gives you a clue. If you cover your sins, you shall not prosper. But if you confess them and forsake them, you shall have mercy. "He that covereth his sins shall not prosper but whoso confesseth and forsaketh them shall have mercy."

Yes, Jesus has already paid the price for our deliverance and freedom. However, it does require an effort on our part to walk and live in this freedom. "Let us labor to enter into that rest" (Hebrews 4:11, KJV). We must take the necessary steps to ensure we are right with God. We can ask God to shine His Holy Spirit spot light on our hearts and see if there is anything in us that is not pleasing to Him and make sure we get it right with God - things like strife, unforgiveness, bitterness, guilt or any other open door that would keep us in bondage.

GUILT:

Here is one example of a spirit of guilt that was in a man I prayed for from Thailand. He was suffering with tormenting thoughts of suicide and playing Russian roulette. He was also involved with pornography and had a lot of anger and rage. While talking with him and finding out the legal authority the enemy (demonic entities) had in his life, before we were about to pray for him, I also sensed to ask him the question, "have you ever been involved with an abortion?" As soon as I asked him the question he manifested violently then jumped down into a position with his legs crossed and had a look about him like a Buddha statue - a stone look about him.

After praying for him and then talking to him, he let us know that years ago his girlfriend had an abortion; he drove her to get the abortion and he always felt so guilty about it.

Not only was the act of being involved with abortion an open door to the enemy but the fact that he was holding so much guilt and so much shame was destroying his life and his family.

After he forgave himself and these spirits of anger, rage, death, and suicide were cast out, he was so thankful to God for his freedom in Christ. He was free from the bondage of sin and death. He knows who his redeemer is, and he gladly shares the Good news of Jesus with others today.

Once we come to our Heavenly Father, God, and receive Him as our Lord and Savior and ask Him to forgive us for ALL of our sins, He does. His love and His mercy endures forever.

SELF HATRED:
Once we were ministering to a man I will call his name Titus, (which is not his real name), that hated his self and did not know how to be free from the guilt of the horrible acts that he did which I will not mention in this book. He served years in prison for those crimes

and although he was free from the physical prison he remained in his own mental/emotional/spiritual prison. It is amazing the number of people that we minister to that have self-hatred and do not want to forgive themselves. We led him to understand the importance of receiving God's love and the great mercy that He has for all humanity.

The demon started to manifest and say he does not want to come out and, "he is my friend, we have been friends a long time" and "he has so much work to do for me." "I don't want to go; if I go out, I am only going to return when he stops following the Word." After we cast out many devils one of the demons inside said, "all my friends are leaving." I also asked him if he had any nicknames in the past and found out that he actually had three multiple personalities.

He also had a spirit of fear that manifested saying, "He has a lot of fear. That is why he is not successful; he is afraid." We cast out the spirit of fear as well.

There was this one stubborn devil that wanted to stay in Titus, so I asked Titus, "Did you ever intentionally invite demons inside of you?" And he confessed that he was looking on the internet one day and was reading some things about Satan and sold his soul to the devil, and he signed his name to it but he did not take it seriously.

So, I told him since he invited the devil into him, that he should tell the evil spirit to leave him in the name of Jesus and he canceled the contract that he signed with the devil in the name of Jesus and he asked God to forgive him for doing that and once he does, his sins are washed in the blood of Jesus and the enemy has no legal authority in his life. He has confessed his sins, then he has renounced it (meaning he will no longer have anything to do with it, he has turned his back on the sin), he is forgiven. I shared with him that God said in His Word that he must forgive himself.

We started to pray for him again and the demon said, "I have been here twenty-three years." I told Titus that he needed to let the guilt and shame go, and don't hold on to it. He started sobbing bitterly with such tears of sadness and regret and hopelessness and cried out, "How do I do that? How do I get rid of the guilt? How do I let it goooooo?" I said, "Forgive yourself, release yourself from the guilt, and know that it is washed away in the powerful blood of Jesus. And God said he washes our sins away as far as the East is from the West and He does not remember our sins anymore." We led Titus to say, "I forgive myself, I release myself from all guilt and condemnation." And he meant it. The last demon before he left said, "there is too much peace in here." So we prayed in the name of Jesus the Christ of Nazareth, "Come out of him," and he did. Titus was free!

Once we come to our Heavenly Father, God, and receive Him as our Lord and Savior and ask Him to forgive us for ALL of our sins, He does. It is about submitting our lives to God (following His Word to love), resisting the devil (that includes in our thoughts) and he will flee. God's love and mercy endures forever.

We need to exorcise our love and mature in our spiritual growth and development of our new freedom in Jesus Christ. Love God, love people, and love our selves.

I have many true stories when I ministered deliverance and the Kingdom of God was at hand. Many captives were gloriously set free by the power of God. It is all His power, and all the glory belongs to God. The Lord Jesus Christ He is the deliverer.

CHAPTER TWENTY

Quotes by Famous People

Mel Gibson:
1. "It's a wise man who understands that every day is a new beginning, because boy, how many mistakes do you make in a day? I don't know about you, but I make plenty. You can't turn the clock back, so you have to look ahead."
2. "The Holy Ghost was working through me on this film, and I was just directing traffic."

Denzel Washington:
1. "You pray for rain, you gotta deal with the mud too. That's a part of it.
2. "I made a commitment to completely cut out drinking and anything that might hamper me from getting my mind and body together. And the floodgates of goodness have opened upon me - spiritually and financially."

3. "If you have an enemy, then learn and know your enemy, don't just be mad at him or her."
4. "My faith helps me understand that circumstances don't dictate my happiness, my inner peace."

Salena Gomez:
1. "We only have one life, and it is very precious, and there's a lot we can do, and there's a lot we should do."
2. "If you are broken, you do not have to stay broken."

Stephen Baldwin:
1. "Evolution isn't true, because if we evolved from monkeys, how can they still be here?"
2. "Demons manifest themselves in people in different ways. For instance, out of nowhere, somebody can become very angry for no reason. That's not just an emotion. That's a demon."
3. "I'm not going to fight in the physical with physical weapons, because it's not a physical fight. I'm going to fight with spiritual weapons, cause it's a spiritual fight."
4. "Loving Jesus is what's most important to me. I know it sounds hokey, but it's the truth."

Cuba Gooding, Jr.:
> Don't let people disrespect you. My mom says don't open the door to the devil. Surround yourself with positive people."

Dwayne Johnson:
> "I think there are a number of things that you can do to encourage your kids' dreams, but I do believe in speaking by experience of having a lot of help along the way, stumbling in the past. We've all stumbled, and we certainly all deserve to get up and walk again."

James Cavizel:
1. "I always believed in God, I would go to mass most of the time, but I had no idea of the calling to holiness.
2. "We are all culpable in the death of Christ. My sins, your sins put Him on that cross.
3. "The point I'm trying to make is that you go to church on Sunday. But the real Christ is out there in your life every day, whether it be the guy you help on the street, how you live your life, and your countenance that makes people want to be you."

Justin Beiber:
>"The way I look at God and my relationship with Jesus is I'm not trying to earn God's love by doing good things. God has already loved me for who I am before I did anything to earn or deserve it. It's a free gift by accepting Jesus, giving your life to him, and what he did is the gift." (Feb 2020 disrn.com)

Steve Harvey:
>"I'm just a living witness that you can be an imperfect soldier and still be in the army fighting for God Almighty. Don't you think you got to be perfect 'cause I ain't." (inspiringquotes.us)

Tim Tebow:
1. "You and I were created by God to be so much more than normal...Following the crowd is not a winning approach to life. In the end it's a loser's game, because we never become who God created us to be by trying to be like everybody else."
2. "For me, my goal is to be able to impact as many people as possible for something good, for something right; to be able to leave a legacy of something bigger than myself - not for winning games, not for scoring touchdowns, but that Jesus Christ has changed my life. You can love

God, and you can love people. There's more to this world than money, fame, and power. You can have an impact, no matter who you are; no matter what platform. No matter how big or small of a role model, there's someone watching you. There's a life that you can change. There's a life that you can impact."

3. "I don't know what my future holds, but I do know who holds my future."
4. If I didn't work as hard as I could, then I think it would be a bit like saying, 'God, thanks for giving me this ability, but I don't really care about it. I'm going to do something else, and I'm not going to work quite as hard.
5. "Every time I step on the field, I'm going to give my whole heart regardless of the score."
6. "Along the way there's going to be a lot of obstacles, a lot of adversity, a lot of people who will tell you you're not good enough. I'm here to tell you that you are. Everyone that tells you that you're not is because they didn't accomplish something."
7. "I want to make someone's life better because I'm here. If you have that attitude it will change your day and change your life."
8. "Where we start to lose it is when we start to grasp onto what we think is ours. No, this is

mine. No, that's my career. That's my money. That's my platform. But really, no, It's yours, God. It's not mine. You might lend it to me for a little while. You might let me hold onto it. You might let me use it for a little bit, but that's not mine; it's yours. Thank you for letting me use that for a little while. I think that's what staying grounded means."

Dr. Martin Luther King, Jr.:
1. "Darkness cannot drive out darkness; only light can do that. Hate cannot drive out hate; only love can do that."
2.
3. "Use me, God. Show me how to take who I am, who I want to be, and what I can do, and use it for a purpose greater than myself."
4. "Be the Peace You Wish To See In The World!"
5. "Not everybody can be famous but everybody can be great, because greatness is determined by service."
6. "Life's most persistent and urgent question is, 'What are you doing for others?'"
7. "Never forget that everything Hitler did in Germany was legal."
8. "The time is always right to do what is right."

9. "I have decided to stick with love. Hate is too great a burden to bear."
10. "I am convinced that love is the most durable power in the world. It is not an expression of impractical idealism, but of practical realism. Far from being the pious injunction of a Utopian dreamer, love is an absolute necessity for the survival of our civilization. To return hate for hate does nothing but intensify the existence of evil in the universe. Someone must have sense enough and religion enough to cut off the chain of hate and evil, and this can only be done through love."
11. "Let us not seek to satisfy our thirst for freedom by drinking from the cup of bitterness and hatred."
12. "The first question which the priest and the Levite asked was: 'If I stop to help this man, what will happen to me?' But... the good Samaritan reversed the question: 'If I do not stop to help this man, what will happen to him?'"
13. "Perhaps the worst sin in life is knowing right and not doing it."
14. Jesus Christ was an extremist for love, truth and goodness."
15. "Forgiveness is not an occasional act, it is a constant attitude.

16. "A productive and happy life is not something you find; it is something you make."
17. "In the End, we will remember not the words of our enemies but the silence of our friends."
18. Was not Jesus an extremist in love? - "Love your enemies, bless them that curse you, pray for them that despitefully use you."
19. "To ignore evil is to become an accomplice to it."
20. "We must discover the power of love, the power, the redemptive power of love. And when we discover that we will be able to make of this old world a new world. We will be able to make men better. Love is the only way."

Billy Graham: (BillyGrahamLibrary.org)

1. "I suppose the most misused word in all the English language is the word 'Love.' But, you know, the whole Bible is a love story; God's love affair with the human race."
2. "I want you to know tonight one thing: God loves you. No matter how you've lived and no matter what the color of your skin; no matter what your racial background, no matter what language you speak – God loves you!"
3. "God's love is unchangeable; He knows exactly what we are and loves us anyway."

4. "True love is an act of the will – a conscious decision to do what is best for the other person instead of ourselves."
5. "The one badge of Christian discipleship is not orthodoxy but love." (upjourney.com)

Ann Graham Lotz:
1. "When the storms of life come, if they come to me personally, to my family or to the world, I want to be strong enough to stand and be a strength to somebody else, be shelter for somebody else."
2. "Abraham wasn't perfect. He failed, made mistakes. But he would go back, get right with God, and then just keep moving forward. He didn't quit when things got hard. He just kept on going. And everywhere he went, God was there. God was with him."
3. "I believe that God has a plan and purpose not only for the human race, but for my individual life."

Oprah Winfrey:
1. "Real integrity is doing the right thing, knowing that nobody's going to know whether you did it or not."
2. "Cheers to a new year and another chance for us to get it right."

3. "The struggle of my life created empathy - I could relate to pain, being abandoned, having people not love me.
4. "I believe that every single event in life happens in an opportunity to choose love over fear."
5. "Love somebody. Just one person. And then spread that to two. And as many as you can. You'll see the difference it makes."
6. "What material success does is provide you with the ability to concentrate on other things that really matter. And that is being able to make a difference, not only in your own life, but in other people's lives."
7. "The thing you fear most has no power. Your fear of it is what has the power. Facing the truth really will set you free."
8. "Money is worth nothing if it can't buy you the opportunity to love more."
9. "Whatever has happened to you in your past has no power over this present moment, because life is now."
10. "When you forgive somebody, it doesn't necessarily mean you want to invite them to your table."
11. "To me, the money is - it's certainly a wonderful thing. But it is in direct proportion to how you're able to bless yourself and bless others with it."

Paula White Cain:

1. "Don't waste another moment crying over what went wrong! If it wasn't a blessing - it was a lesson."
2. "God takes what the enemy meant for your bad and turns it for your good! It wasn't a set back but a set up! Wait and see what God is getting ready to do for you!"
3. "Someone's opinion of you isn't reality... unless you decide to allow it!! You are who God says you are!!!"
4. "I say you have to remember in darkness what he told you in light. And the principle is this that there are times that it does feel like God is playing hide and go seek. But I trust him."
5. "Satisfaction comes from the inside out, so people keep gravitating from things externally to try to fill something - get a man to complete them, get money to complete them, get a job to complete them and still find themselves frustrated."

Joel Osteen:

1. "When you go through difficult times, make sure you pass the test. Don't be stubborn and hardheaded. Recognize that God is refining you, knocking off some of your rough edges. Stand strong and fight the good fight of faith. God

has called each of us to be champions; you are destined to win. If you will work with God and keep a good attitude, then no matter what comes against you, the bible says that all things – not just the good things in life, but all things – work together for your good."
2. "The more you talk about negative things in your life, the more you call them in. Speak victory not defeat."
3. "Your destiny is not determined by your critics. Focus on running your own race."
4. "Don't use your words to describe the situation. Use your words to change the situation."
5. "I don't have to figure out how God is going to solve my problem. I don't have to understand how He's going to bring it to pass. That's His responsibility. My job is to simply believe that He will."
6. "You spend your time like you spend money. You can waste it or invest it."
7. "The only difference between black coal and a precious diamond is the amount of pressure it endured."

Albert Einstein:

"If we knew what it was we were doing, it would not be called research, would it?"

Kenneth Copeland:
1. "You can foul up the devil's whole strategy by taking charge of your thoughts and bringing them in line with the Word of God."
2. "What comes out of our hearts through the words of our mouths determines what comes to pass in our lives. It's the absolute truth."

Joyce Meyer: (AZQuotes.com)
1. "A positive attitude gives you power over your circumstances instead of your circumstances having power over you."
2. "Before you judge someone else, stop and think about all that God has forgiven you for."
3. "Battles are fought in our minds every day. When we begin to feel the battle is just too difficult and want to give up, we must choose to resist negative thoughts and be determined to rise above our problems. We must decide that we're not going to quit. When we're bombarded with doubts and fears, we must take a stand and say: "I'll never give up! God's on my side. He loves me, and He's helping me! I'm going to make it!"

Elvis Presley. (Source AZQuotes.com)
1. "Everybody comes from the same source. If you hate another human being, you're hating part of yourself."
2. "To judge a man by his weakest link or deed is like judging the power of the ocean by one wave."
3. "Truth is like the sun. You can shut it out for a time, but it ain't goin' away."
4. "Love had surely made us all and hate would surely make us fall."

Mother Teresa:
1. "The hunger for love is much more difficult to remove than the hunger for bread."
2. "Even the rich are hungry for love, for being cared for, for being wanted, for having someone to call their own."
3. "Let us more and more insist on raising funds of love, of kindness, of understanding, of peace. Money will come if we seek first the Kingdom of God - the rest will be given."
4. "Spread love everywhere you go. Let no one ever come to you without leaving happier."
5. "If you judge people, you have no time to love them."
6. "Love begins by taking care of the closest ones - the ones at home."

7. "Intense love does not measure, it just gives."
8. "There is more hunger for love and appreciation in this world than for bread."
9. "Let us not be satisfied with just giving money. Money is not enough, money can be got, but they need your hearts to love them. So, spread your love everywhere you go."
10. "Spread love everywhere you go; first of all in your house. Give love to your children, to your wife or husband, to a next-door neighbor. Let no one ever come to you without leaving better and happier."
11. "The greatest disease in the West today is not TB or leprosy; it is being unwanted, unloved, and uncared for. We can cure physical diseases with medicine, but the only cure for loneliness, despair, and hopelessness is love. There are many in the world who are dying for a piece of bread but there are many more dying for a little love. The poverty in the West is a different kind of poverty -- it is not only a poverty of loneliness but also of spirituality. There's a hunger for love, as there is a hunger for God."
12. "Love cannot remain by itself - it has no meaning. Love has to be put into action and that action is service."

13. "It is easy to love the people far away. It is not always easy to love those close to us. It is easier to give a cup of rice to relieve hunger than to relieve the loneliness and pain of someone unloved in our own home. Bring love into your home for this is where our love for each other must start."
14. "Give your hands to serve and your hearts to love."
15. "We can cure physical diseases with medicine, but the only cure for loneliness, despair, and hopelessness is love. There are many in the world who are dying for a piece of bread, but there are many more dying for a little love."
16. "When Christ said: I was hungry and you fed me, he didn't mean only the hunger for bread and for food; he also meant the hunger to be loved. Jesus himself experienced this loneliness. He came amongst his own and his own received him not, and it hurt him then and it has kept on hurting him. The same hunger, the same loneliness, the same having no one to be accepted by and to be loved and wanted by. Every human being in that case resembles Christ in his loneliness; and that is the hardest part, that's real hunger."
17. "If you think well of others, you will also speak well of others and to others. From the abundance

of the heart the mouth speaks. If your heart is full of love, you will speak of love."
18. "There is always the danger that we may just do the work for the sake of the work. This is where the respect and the love and the devotion come in - that we do it to God, to Christ, and that's why we try to do it as beautifully as possible."
19. "I will never tire of repeating this: what the poor need the most is not pity but love. They need to feel respect for their human dignity, which is neither less nor different from the dignity of any other human being."
20. "In each of our lives Jesus comes as the Bread of Life - to be eaten, to be consumed by us. This is how He loves us. Then Jesus comes in our human life as the hungry one, the other, hoping to be fed with the Bread of our life, our hearts by loving, and our hands by serving. In loving and serving, we prove that we have been created in the likeness of God, for God is Love and when we love we are like God. This is what Jesus meant when He said, "Be perfect as your Father in heaven is perfect."
21. "There are some people who, in order not to pray use as an excuse the fact that life is so hectic that it prevents us from praying. This cannot be. Prayer does not demand that we interrupt our

work, but that we continue working as if it were a prayer. It is not necessary to always be in meditation, nor to consciously experience the sensation that we are talking to God, no matter how nice that would be. What matters is being with Him, living in Him, in His will. To love with a pure heart, to love everybody, especially to live the poor, is a twenty-four-hour prayer."
22. "God loves the world through us."

Conclusion

The church of Jesus Christ is still being confronted by the same opposition of demon power that confronted the church of the New Testament. We have the anointing of the Holy Spirit and we must understand that we have authority and power over our adversary as in the Scriptures. We have the name and the blood of the Lord Jesus Christ.

Throughout God's Word, He tells us that sin will allow an open door for the enemy to have access in our lives. We are under Grace in the New Covenant; however, we are to live sanctified lives unto the Lord and walk in His ways. The way of Love.

Love is the completeness of God's nature. If we want to be more like Him, we need to be love too. God is so merciful and yet He requires us to forgive everyone and even though you are releasing them from their offenses the person that really gains freedom is the one that forgives and loves.

It is God's will to heal and deliver ALL those oppressed of the devil. Jesus commissioned us, His people, to tell the world about Him, to cast out devils in His name, and heal the sick. We, His people, are to set the captives free all for His glory.

Freedom requires an effort. We must submit to God, submit to His Word, live a life of love, then we can resist the devil and he will flee. We have the Holy Spirit in us, and He will give us the power to overcome.

We love, not because we are Christians and you have to, but because it is who you are. By this will all men know that you are My disciples, if you have love one to another.

Bibliography

Bevere, John, *Bait of Satan*, Lake Mary, Florida: Charisma House, 2004.

Greenwood, Rebecca, *Let Our Children Go*, Lake Mary, Florida: Charisma House, 2011.

Hagin, Kenneth E., *The Believer's Authority*, Broken Arrow, Oklahoma: Faith Library Publications, 1986.

Hagin, Kenneth, *Following God's Plan for Your Life*, Broken Arrow, Oklahoma: Rhema Bible Church, 1993.

Hagin, Kenneth E., *Triumphant Church*, Broken Arrow, Oklahoma: Rhema Bible Church, 1993.

Hayes, Norval, *How To Live and Not Die*, Tulsa, Oklahoma: Harrison House, 1986.

Henderson, Robert, *Operating In The Courts of Heaven*, Midlothian, Texas: Robert Henderson Ministries, 2014.

Howard-Browne, Rodney M., *How to Increase The Anointing*, Tampa, Florida: RMI Publications, 1995.

Kenyon, E. W., *The Blood Covenant*, Lynnwood, Washington: Kenyon's Gospel Publishing Society, 36th Printing 2012.

Kraft, Charles, *I Give You Authority*, Ada, Michigan: Chosen Books, 2009.

Prince, Derek, *Expelling Demons*, Charlotte, North Carolina: Derek Prince Ministries, 1970.

Renner, Rick, *Dream Thieves*, Colorado Springs, Colorado: Teach All Nations, 2009.

Renner, Rick, *Dressed to Kill*, Tulsa, Oklahoma: Harrison House, 1991.

Stone, Perry, *Exposing Satan's Playbook*, Lake Mary, Florida: Charisma House, 2012.

Wigglesworth, Smith, *On Spiritual Gifts*, Tulsa, Oklahoma: Harrison House, 1998.

Wright, Henry W., *A More Excellent Way*, New Kensington, Pennsylvania: Whitaker House, 1999.

Wright, Henry W., *From the Inside Out*, Thomaston, Georgia: Be in Health, 2007.

Wright, Henry W., *Insights into Addictions*, Thomaston, Georgia: Be in Health, 2007.

Yandian, Bob, *Ephesians A New Testament Commentary*, Tulsa, Oklahoma: Harrison House Publishers, 2016.

CPSIA information can be obtained
at www.ICGtesting.com
Printed in the USA
BVHW041550180121
598053BV00011B/974